Claus und Sally Vollmers

Speak! Phone! Write!

Berufsvorbereitungsjahr

Geschäftsenglisch für Anfänger und Lernende mit geringen Vorkenntnissen

1. Auflage

Bestellnummer 11311

Bildungsverlag EINS
a Wolters Kluwer business

www.bildungsverlag1.de

Bildungsverlag EINS
Sieglarer Straße 2, 53842 Troisdorf

ISBN 978-3-427-**11311**-9

Vorwort

Speak! Phone! Write! ist für alle gedacht, die Englisch beruflich benötigen, aber über keine oder nur sehr geringe Kenntnisse der Sprache verfügen.

In fast allen Stellenanzeigen wird „Englisch in Wort und Schrift" verlangt. Sobald Sie mit Englisch sprechenden Kollegen oder Kunden zu tun haben, ist es unabdingbar, dass Sie mit diesen kommunizieren können. Dafür müssen Sie sich verschiedene Fähigkeiten aktiv aneignen, um einerseits zu verstehen, was man Ihnen sagt und um sich andererseits verständlich machen zu können.

Jede „Unit" (Lektion) ist in drei Hauptteile gegliedert: *Speak!, Phone!* und *Write!* Die Lernziele für jede Unit finden sich am Anfang der Unterkapitel. Wenn Sie alle diese Ziele erreichen, werden Sie in Zukunft auch in einer Englisch sprechenden Umgebung gute Arbeit leisten können.

Damit Sie Ihr Gehör trainieren und Ihre eigene Aussprache kontrollieren können, gibt es jeden Hörtext – im Buch durch ein CD-Icon gekennzeichnet – auf der beiliegenden Audio-CD zum Anhören. Machen Sie von diesem Angebot reichlich Gebrauch, die meisten Hörtexte können Sie gleichzeitig mitlesen. Die Hörtexte, die Sie nicht abgedruckt finden, sind als Hörverständnisübungen konzipiert: Hier konzentrieren Sie sich nur auf das Verstehen des Gehörten – und zwar so intensiv, dass Sie die dazu erstellten Fragen beantworten können.

Am wichtigsten ist es natürlich, eigene Ideen kommunizieren zu können. Deshalb gibt es viele Übungen, die Sie gemeinsam mit einem Partner lösen können. Diese Aufgaben sind – ebenfalls per Icon – als „Partnerarbeit" gekennzeichnet.

Sie dürfen ruhig mit einem deutschen Akzent Englisch sprechen, solange man Sie leicht verstehen kann. Sie sollten nicht versuchen, sich erst auf Deutsch einen Satz auszudenken, um diesen dann anschließend ins Englische zu übersetzen. Verwenden Sie einfache, sowie kurze englische Sätze. Am Anfang werden Sie trotzdem auch einige Fehler machen: Dadurch werden Sie aber lernen! Lassen Sie sich also nicht entmutigen und niemals vom Sprechen abhalten.

Für die selbstständige Formulierung von Sätzen benötigen Sie einige Regeln, die den Satzaufbau im Englischen festlegen. Zu diesem Zweck sind innerhalb der Lektionen immer wieder kleine Grammatikpassagen eingeflochten. Prüfen Sie sich selbst, ob Sie die Regeln richtig verstanden haben, indem Sie die entsprechenden Grammatikübungen bearbeiten. Danach haben Sie die Gelegenheit, die nun erlernten Strukturen mündlich und schriftlich anzuwenden. Die Anweisungen zu den Übungen (Exercises) sind zum besseren Verständnis sowohl auf Englisch als auch auf Deutsch angegeben.

Ohne einen bestimmten Wortschatz einschließlich gebräuchlicher Redewendungen, finden Sie sich im Berufsalltag nicht gut zurecht. Die jede Lektion abschließende „Vocabulary Practice" unterstützt Sie auf diesem wichtigen Gebiet. Hier wiederholen Sie die wichtigsten Vokabeln der betreffenden Lektion und am Ende des Buches folgt abschließend eine chronologische sowie eine alphabetische Wörterliste. Wenn Sie eine Vokabel nicht kennen, schlagen Sie dort nach.

Contents/Inhaltsverzeichnis

1 Contacts

Speak!

Sie lernen:

sich selbst oder Kollegen vorzustellen,
korrekte Begrüßungsformen zu verwenden,
persönliche Daten zu erfragen und mitzuteilen.

Pleased to meet you

Audio Text 1 | Hörtext 1

1

Read and listen to the text. | Lesen und hören Sie den Text.

Here is the head office of Aquapure Ltd. Aquapure is a British firm. Ann is an employee of Aquapure Ltd and Paul is a new trainee from Germany.

Ann Hello, my name is Ann Jones. What's your name?
Paul My name is Paul Braun. Hello, Ann. Pleased to meet you.
Ann I'm pleased to meet you, Paul.

Business Tip

Wenn Sie sich auf Englisch vorstellen, nennen Sie immer **Vornamen und Nachnamen**. Engländer und Amerikaner ziehen es vor, Geschäftspartner gleich mit Vornamen anzureden.
Vorsicht: Viele Geschäftsleute aus anderen Ländern, zum Beispiel aus Asien, sprechen zwar Englisch als Geschäftssprache, erwarten aber nicht, mit Vornamen angeredet zu werden.

2

Where are you from?

Audio Text 2 | Hörtext 2

Read and listen to the text. Answer the questions below. | Lesen und hören Sie den Text. Beantworten Sie die darunter stehenden Fragen.

Ann Where are you from, Paul?
Paul I'm from Berlin.
Ann Pardon? What? Please say that again. Where are you from?
Paul I'm from Berlin.
Ann From Berlin? Oh! Are you German?
Paul Yes, that is right. I'm from Germany. Where are you from? Are you from Leeds?
Ann No, I'm not from Leeds. I am from Otley, a village near Leeds. I'm an assistant manager in the sales department.
Paul Oh. I'm new here. I'm a trainee. I'm in the sales department, too.

Exercise

1 Give the English for: | Übersetzen Sie ins Englische:

a) Erfreut, Sie kennenzulernen.
b) Ich heiße Paul.
c) Mein Name ist Paul.
d) Wie bitte?
e) Ich komme nicht aus Leeds.

Bitte sagen Sie das noch mal.
Bist du aus Berlin?
Woher kommst du?*
Woher kommen Sie?*
Woher kommt ihr?*

(* Auf Englisch: du, Sie und ihr = you!)

And you!

Introduce yourself. | Stellen Sie sich vor.

Ask where your partner is from. | Fragen Sie, woher Ihr Partner kommt.
Say where you are from. | Sagen Sie, woher Sie kommen.

Grammar

Short forms | Kurzformen

So spricht man (Kurzform):
I'm in London.
I'm/you're/we're in London.
He's/she's/it's in London.
They're in London.

So schreibt man (Langform):
I am in London.
I am/you are/we are in London.
He is/she is/it is in London.
They are in London.

Exercise

2 Write the short forms | Verwenden Sie die Kurzformen

a) I am from Germany.
b) You are English.
c) Berlin is in Germany.
d) It is a big city.
e) Ann is from Otley.
f) She is a sales assistant.
g) Paul is German.
h) He is from Berlin.
i) They are in Leeds.
j) They are at work now.

3 Fill in the gaps: **am, is,** or **are** | Füllen Sie die Lücken: **am, is,** oder **are**

a) You ______ a trainee.
b) I ______ English.
c) Leeds ______ a city in England.
d) Ann ______ at work.
e) Paul ______ new here.
f) John ______ the sales director.
g) John, Paul and Ann ______ in the office.
h) Ann and Paul ______ talking to John.

4 Replace the underlined words with **he/she/it** or **they**. | Ersetzen Sie die unterstrichenen Wörter durch **he/she/it** oder **they**.

a) Ann is from Leeds. Ann is an assistant manager.
b) Paul is new. Paul is German.
c) Paul is from Berlin.
d) Ann and Paul are in the office now.
e) The office is in Leeds, a city in the North of England.
f) Leeds is a big city. Manchester is a big city, too.
g) But Manchester and Leeds are not as big as London.
h) Here is the sun! The sun is hot!

Negatives | Verneinungen

	Long form (Langform)	Short form (Kurzform)		
I am	I am not	I'm not		
You/we are	You/we are not	You/we aren't	*oder*	you're/ we're not
He/she/it is	He/she/it is not	He/she/it isn't	*oder*	he's/she's/it's not
They are	They are not	They aren't	*oder*	they're not

Exercise

5 Make the negative sentence. | Verneinen Sie.

a) She is my friend.
b) It is hot.
c) We are busy.
d) They are here.
e) The boss is happy.
f) You are late.
g) He is the new trainee.
h) They are from France.
i) I am a secretary.

6 Give the answers. | **Beantworten Sie die Fragen.**

Example/Beispiel

Is Paul from Berlin?	Yes, he is.
Is Ann from London?	No, she isn't.

a) Is Leeds in England?
b) Are Paul and Ann in London?
c) Is London a small city?
d) Is Paul a girl?
e) Is Paris in Germany?
f) Are Paul and Ann in Japan?
g) Is the Eiffel Tower in Tokyo?

And you!

Ask and answer similar questions. | **Stellen und beantworten Sie ähnliche Fragen.**

Business Tip

Plc (Public limited company) und Ltd (limited liability) sind Rechtsformen britischer Unternehmen. Eine „plc" ist ein Unternehmen mit beschränkter Haftung, dessen Aktien an der Börse gehandelt werden können. Die Ltd (limited company) ist ein privates Unternehmen mit beschränkter Haftung, das nicht an der Börse notiert ist.

Meet the boss!

Audio Text 3 | Hörtext 3

3

Read and listen to the text and answer the questions. | **Lesen und hören Sie den Text und beantworten Sie die Fragen.**

Ann and Paul are in John Smith's office. John is the sales director. He is Ann's boss.

John Hello, Ann. How are you today?
Ann Good morning, John. I'm fine, thanks. This is the new trainee from Germany, Paul Braun. Paul, this is John Smith. He is our boss. He is the sales director.
John How do you do, Paul?
Paul Pleased to meet you, Mr Smith.
John Please call me John!
Paul OK, thanks, John.
John And how are you, Paul?
Paul I'm fine, thanks, and you?
John I'm fine.

Exercise

7 Right or wrong? Correct if wrong. | Richtig oder falsch? Korrigieren Sie die Fehler.

Example/Beispiel

Paul is a trainee from Germany. That is right.
Paul is a trainee from France. No, he isn't from France. He is from Germany.

a) Mr Smith is the finance director.
b) Paul and Ann are employees of Aquapure Ltd.
c) Paul's family name is Braun.
d) Ann is from Hamburg.
e) Paul is Ann's boss.
f) Leeds is in Germany.
g) Ann is a secretary.

And you!

Play the roles of John, Ann and Paul. Use your own names. | **Spielen Sie die Rollen von John, Ann und Paul. Setzen Sie dabei ihre eigenen Namen ein.**

Business Tip

Einige Leute sagen "How do you do?" statt "Pleased to meet you".
"How do you do?" ist keine richtige Frage. Es bedeutet dasselbe wie "Pleased to meet you": „Erfreut, Sie kennenzulernen".
Man antwortet auch mit: "How do you do?" oder "Pleased to meet you."
"How are you?" heißt „Wie geht es Ihnen/dir?". Mögliche Antwort: "Fine, thanks".
Vorsicht: Auch wenn man den Chef mit Vornamen anspricht, heißt das nicht, dass man ihm gegenüber weniger respektvoll sein darf.

Grammar

"a" or "an" | "a" oder "an"

a + Mitlaut: a man/a city

an + Selbstlaut: an assistant/an office

Vor **Berufsbezeichnungen** steht im Englischen "a" oder "an".

I'm **a** teacher. — Ich **bin** Lehrerin.

I'm **an** assistant manager. — Ich **bin** Assistent/-in der Geschäftsführung.

Exercise

8 What is it in German? | Wie heißt das auf Deutsch?

• office worker • secretary • translator • interpreter • accountant • head of department • programmer • technician • salesman • saleswoman • English teacher • receptionist • trainee • director • bank clerk

"a" or "an"? | "a" oder "an"?

a) They are in ______ office.
b) She is ______ English teacher.
c) He is ______ French teacher.
d) That is ______ American book.
e) This is ______ British text.
f) This is ______ Italian book.

And you!

Ask and answer. | Fragen und antworten Sie.

a) What is your job? — I'm a/an ______
b) What is your husband's/father's job? — He's a/an ______
c) What is your wife's/mother's job? — She's a/an ______
d) What is your friend's job? — He's/she's a/an ______

Business Tip

Für die meisten Berufsbezeichnungen gibt es nur eine Form: *doctor, teacher, manager, driver, professor* können alle Mann oder Frau sein. Die Ausnahmen sind: *waiter/waitress* (Kellner/Kellnerin) und *actor/actress* (Schauspieler/Schauspielerin).

Exercise

9 Ask and answer. | Fragen und antworten Sie.

Example/Beispiel

______ you Japanese? — Are you Japanese? No, I'm not.

a) ______ Paris in Germany?
b) ______ London in Germany?
c) ______ you in London?
d) ______ Queen Elizabeth in Berlin?
e) ______ Paul Braun from Sidney?
f) ______ Ann in London?

10 Ask the questions. | Stellen Sie die Fragen.

Example/Beispiel

My name is Ann. — *What/name?* — *What is your name?*

a) I'm from Liverpool. — Where/from?
b) Yes, it is. — Liverpool/in England?
c) No, I'm not. I'm British. — You/German?
d) Jane? No, she isn't my secretary. — Jane/your secretary?
e) She is from Manchester. — Where/she/from?

And you!

Ask and answer in English. | Fragen und antworten Sie auf Englisch.

a) Wie geht es dir?
b) Wie heißen Sie?
c) Woher kommen Sie?
d) Sind Sie Amerikaner?
e) Bist du Deutsche?
f) Bist du aus England?

Grammar

Pronouns | Pronomen

Im Englischen gibt es nur ein Wort für du/dich/dir/ihr/euch/Sie und Ihnen: you.

Personal pronoun/Personalpronomen		Possessive pronoun/Possessivpronomen	
I	ich	my	mein
you	du	your	dein
he	er	his	sein
she	sie	her	ihr
it	es	its	sein
we	wir	our	unser
you	ihr, Sie	your	euer
they	sie	their	ihr

I am at **my** desk.
You are at **your** desk(s).
He is at **his** desk.
She is at **her** desk.
It is on the desk.
We are at **our** desks.
They are at **their** desks.

Exercise

11 Replace the underlined words with pronouns. | Ersetzen Sie die unterstrichenen Wörter durch Pronomen.

• he • she • it • they

a) Paul is from Berlin.
b) Berlin is a city in Germany.
c) His sister is a secretary.
d) Paul and Ann are in the office.
e) The office is in Leeds.
f) The trainees are in the office.

12 Complete the dialogue. | Ergänzen Sie den Dialog.

• am • are • I • is • it • you

Paul ___ you from Leeds?
Jane Yes, I ___
Paul ___ you a trainee?
Jane No, I'm a secretary. Are ___ a trainee?
Paul Yes.
Jane And where ___ ___ from?
Paul Berlin.
Jane Oh. Berlin ___ a very nice city!
Paul Yes, ___ ___. But Leeds ___ nice, too.
Jane Well yes, ___ is OK. But Berlin ___ better!

Exercise

13 Complete the sentences. | Ergänzen Sie die Sätze.

• her • his • my • our • their • your

a) Who is that man? ______ name is Brian.
b) I am at ______ desk.
c) Hello. What is ______ name.
d) Are Paul and Ann in ______ office? John Smith is ______ boss.
e) This is Ann. ______ hair is brown.
f) This is Paul. ______ eyes are blue.
g) Ann: "We are in the sales department. John Smith is ______ boss".

Plural of nouns | **Mehrzahl des Hauptworts**

Regelmäßig = Wort + s

• girl/girls • boy/boys • trainee/trainees

Wörter, die auf -y enden: Selbstlaut (a, o, i ,e, u) + y:

• boy/boys • day/days

Mitlaut + y:

• city/cities • secretary/secretaries

Wörter, die auf einen „Zischlaut" enden: Wort + es:

• watch/watches • bus/buses

Unregelmäßig:

• man/men • woman/women • child/children • mouse/mice

Exercise

14 Give the plural. | Bilden Sie die Mehrzahl.

• man • girl • teacher • bus • city • watch

15 Put in "is" or "are". | Setzen Sie "is" oder "are" ein.

a) The boy ______ in the office.
b) The girls ______ at home.
c) The man ______ in London.
d) The woman ______ in Leeds.
e) My wife ______ a secretary.
f) The men ______ office workers.
g) The mouse ______ on the desk.
h) He ______ a programmer.
i) His children ______ at school.

Now you talk! | Jetzt reden Sie!

1 Who am I?

Introduce yourself in English. | Stellen Sie sich auf Englisch vor.

My name is
I am from
I am (single/married/divorced)
I am a/an (secretary/salesman/assistant)
My hobby is/My hobbies are
My favourite singer is

2 Who are you?

Ask about your partner's name, address, job, hobby. | Fragen Sie nach Namen, Adresse, Beruf und Hobby Ihres Partners/Ihrer Partnerin.

What is your ?
?
?
?

My name is
My address is
I am a
My hobby is /
My hobbies are

3 Who is he/she?

Report about your partner. | Berichten Sie über Ihren Partner.

His/her name is
His/her address is
He/she is a
His/her hobby is His/her hobbies are

4 Learning by playing

"Who is it?" | „Wer ist das?"

(Schüler/in X denkt an eine noch lebende Person, die vermutlich allen Anwesenden bekannt ist. Durch Fragen auf Englisch, die nur mit "yes" oder "no" zu beantworten sind, müssen die anderen herausfinden, an wen Schüler/in X denkt.)

Example/Beispiel

Is it a man?	Yes, it is.
Is he from Germany?	Yes, he is.
Is he a sportsman?	Yes, he is.
Is he a racing-driver?	No, he isn't.
Is he a football player?	Yes, he is.
Is it Michael Ballack?	Yes, that is right!

Phone!

Sie lernen:

englischsprachige Anrufe zu beantworten und durchzustellen.
Den Anrufer zu informieren, wenn die erwünschte Person nicht anwesend ist.

4

Ann is on the phone

Audio Text 4 | Hörtext 4

Read and listen to the dialogues. | Lesen und hören Sie die Dialoge.

Dialogue 1

Ann	Hello, Ann Jones speaking, Aquapure Ltd, sales department. How can I help you?
Caller	Can I speak to John Smith, please.
Ann	Yes, one moment, please, I'll connect you.

Dialogue 2

Ann	Good morning, Ann Jones speaking, Aquapure Ltd.
Caller	Oh, hello Ann. Can I speak to Brian, please?
Ann	Sorry, he is not available. He is in a meeting.
Caller	OK. I'll phone him this afternoon. Bye. Have a nice day!
Ann	Goodbye.

Exercise

16 Find the English for: | Finden Sie die englischen Entsprechungen für:

- Am Apparat. • Ich verbinde. • Er ist nicht erreichbar. • Wie kann ich Ihnen helfen?
- Einen Moment bitte. • Ich werde ihn heute Nachmittag anrufen.

Business Tip

Verwenden Sie einen **aufsteigenden Tonfall**, wenn Sie einen Anruf auf Englisch beantworten. So wirken Sie gleich viel freundlicher. Nennen Sie Vor- und Nachnamen, wenn Sie sich melden.

Paul answers the phone

5

Audio Text 5 | Hörtext 5

Read and listen to the dialogues. | **Lesen und hören Sie die Dialoge.**

Dialogue 1

Paul Good afternoon. Paul Braun speaking. How can I help you?
Caller Please put me through to Mr Smith.
Paul One moment please. Sorry, the line is busy. Do you want to hold on, or try later?
Caller Pardon. What? I can't understand you. Please say that again.
Paul The line is busy. Will you hold on, or try later?
Caller I'll call him later. Bye.
Paul Goodbye.

Dialogue 2

Paul Hello. Sales department. How can I help you?
Caller I want to speak to John, please.
Paul Pardon. I can't understand you. Please repeat that. My English is not very good.
Caller I want to speak to John Smith, please.
Paul OK, please hold the line. I'll connect you. Sorry, there is no answer.
Caller I'll send an e-mail.

Exercise

17 Find the English for: | **Finden Sie die englischen Entsprechungen für:**

• Er spricht gerade/Die Leitung ist besetzt. • Wollen Sie warten oder es später versuchen? • Ich möchte bitte mit John sprechen. • Bitte wiederholen Sie das/ Bitte sagen Sie das noch mal. • Er antwortet nicht.

Business Tip

Lernen Sie die Redewendungen, die man am Telefon verwendet, auswendig. Sie werden sie häufig brauchen!

Grammar

"will" | „werden"

Auf Deutsch sagen wir **„Ich verbinde"**; auf Englisch sagt man **"I'll connect you"**.

I'll = Kurzform für **I will = ich werde**

Mit "will" muss man im Englischen aufpassen: **Will** heißt nicht **will/wollen**, sondern **werden**.

Ich werde kommen	heißt	**I will come.**
Ich möchte mit Jane sprechen	heißt	**I want to speak to Jane.**

Exercise

18 Translate. | Übersetzen Sie.

a) Guten Morgen, Paul Braun am Apparat.
b) Ich stelle durch.
c) Tut mir leid, er antwortet nicht.
d) Die Leitung ist besetzt.
e) Bitte probieren Sie es später noch mal.
f) Ich möchte mit Frau Jones sprechen, bitte.
g) Sie ist in einer Besprechung.
h) Bitte warten Sie.
i) Ich werde ihm eine E-Mail schicken.
j) Leider ist er nicht erreichbar.

19 Find the right translations. | Finden Sie die richtigen Übersetzungen.

a) He is not available.
b) I'll connect you.
c) He is at a meeting.
d) Please send an e-mail.
e) Please try later.
f) Please speak slowly.
g) He will ring you back.
h) Speaking.
i) I want to speak to John.

(1) Schicken Sie bitte eine E-Mail.
(2) Bitte sprechen Sie langsam.
(3) Er ist in einer Besprechung.
(4) Er ist nicht erreichbar.
(5) Am Apparat.
(6) Rufen Sie später wieder an.
(7) Ich möchte mit John sprechen.
(8) Ich verbinde.
(9) Er ruft Sie zurück.

Business Tip

Begrüßung im Englischen

Morgens: good morning
Nachmittags: good afternoon (nicht "good day")
Abends: good evening
Wenn man schlafen geht: good night

Now you phone!

Audio Text 6 | Hörtext 6

Translate the German into English. Read the dialogues with a partner, then listen to Audio Text 6.

Übersetzen Sie vom Deutschen ins Englische. Lesen Sie die Dialoge mit einem Partner, danach hören Sie sich Hörtext 6 an.

Dialogue 1

You	Guten Tag. Holiday Hotel, Frankfurt.
Caller	Hello, can I speak to the manager, please?
You	Am Apparat. Wie kann ich Ihnen helfen?
Caller	Hello, how are you? This is Jo Black, from Eurotours, London.
You	Guten Tag, Jo. Wie geht es Ihnen?

Dialogue 2

Caller	Good morning. Can you speak English?
You	Ja, aber mein Englisch ist nicht sehr gut. Bitte sprechen Sie langsam.
Caller	OK. Can you put me through to the sales department, please?
You	Ja, ich verbinde. Tut mir leid, aber da antwortet niemand. Wollen Sie warten?
Caller	No thanks, I'll try later. Bye.
You	Auf Wiederhören!

Dialogue 3

You	Guten Tag, Verkaufsabteilung.
Caller	Andrew Grey, from Greys' Ltd here. Who is that speaking, please?
You	(Geben Sie Ihren Namen an) am Apparat. Hallo, Andrew. Wie geht es Ihnen?
Caller	Hi, I'm fine. And you?
You	Sehr gut, danke. Wie kann ich Ihnen helfen?
Caller	Can I speak to Klaus, please?
You	Tut mir leid. Er ist in einer Besprechung.

Another call

Listening Comprehension: Audio Text 7 | Hörtext 7

Listen to Audio Text 7. Correct what is not true.

Hören Sie sich Hörtext 7 an. Korrigieren Sie, was nicht zutrifft.

a) Paul Braun is calling.
b) Wolfgang is speaking to John Smith.
c) Wolfgang is in Berlin.
d) John is in Berlin, too.
e) Ann is Wolfgang's assistant.
f) Wolfgang will try later.

Write!

Sie lernen:

englische E-Mails zu verstehen und einfache E-Mails zu schreiben.

Writing e-mails in English

Rules I Regeln

The subject line I Die Betreffzeile

Vergessen Sie die Betreffzeile nicht! Möglicherweise wird ihre E-Mail sonst gar nicht gelesen.
Example/Beispiel: Project team meeting, 3 June I Your order number 254/9

Attached files I Anhänge

Schreiben Sie immer eine kurze Begleitmail, wenn Sie per E-Mail Dateien senden, sonst kann es passieren, dass man Ihre E-Mail löscht.
Example/Beispiel: You will find the information in the attached file.

The Greeting I Die Begrüßung

E-Mails können lockerer sein als Geschäftsbriefe.

E-Mails an eine Person: Sie können mit "Hi, Pete" oder "Hello, Jane" anfangen, wenn Sie die Person kennen. Wenn es förmlicher zugehen sollte, nehmen Sie die Begrüßungsformen, die Sie in einem Geschäftsbrief benutzen würden.

E-Mails, die an eine Personengruppe adressiert werden: Sie können entweder jeden einzelnen Empfänger separat anschreiben: "Hi, Mary" oder "Dear Ms Jones" oder die ganze Gruppe begrüßen: "Hi, colleagues!" oder "Dear members of the project group".

The close I Der Schluss

"Best regards" oder "Kind regards"

Nützliche Vokabeln

e-mail address	E-Mail-Adresse	attachment/attached file	Anhang
send	schicken	receive	bekommen
get	bekommen	answer	beantworten
answer	Antwort	Best regards	Mit freundlichen Grüßen
sender	Absender	recipient	Empfänger

Two e-mails

E-Mail 1

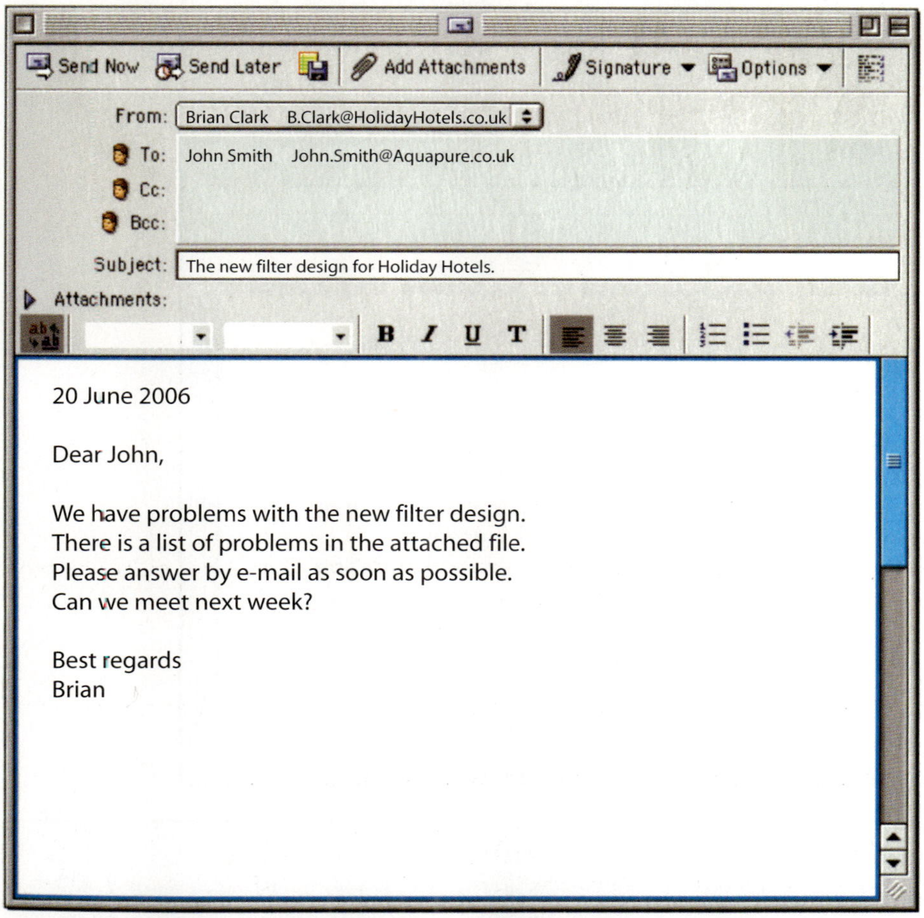

From: Brian Clark B.Clark@HolidayHotels.co.uk
To: John Smith John.Smith@Aquapure.co.uk
Cc:
Bcc:
Subject: The new filter design for Holiday Hotels.
Attachments:

20 June 2006

Dear John,

We have problems with the new filter design.
There is a list of problems in the attached file.
Please answer by e-mail as soon as possible.
Can we meet next week?

Best regards
Brian

Exercise

20 Read the e-mails and answer the questions. | Lesen Sie die E-Mails und beantworten Sie die Fragen.

a) Who is the e-mail to?
b) Who is it from?
c) What is Brian's e-mail address?
d) What is in the attachment?

21 Give the English for: | Übersetzen Sie ins Englische:

• Betrifft • Anhang • Datei • Mit freundlichen Grüßen • so bald wie möglich

Business Tip

Oft schreibt man "asap" als Kurzform für "as soon as possible".

E-mail 2

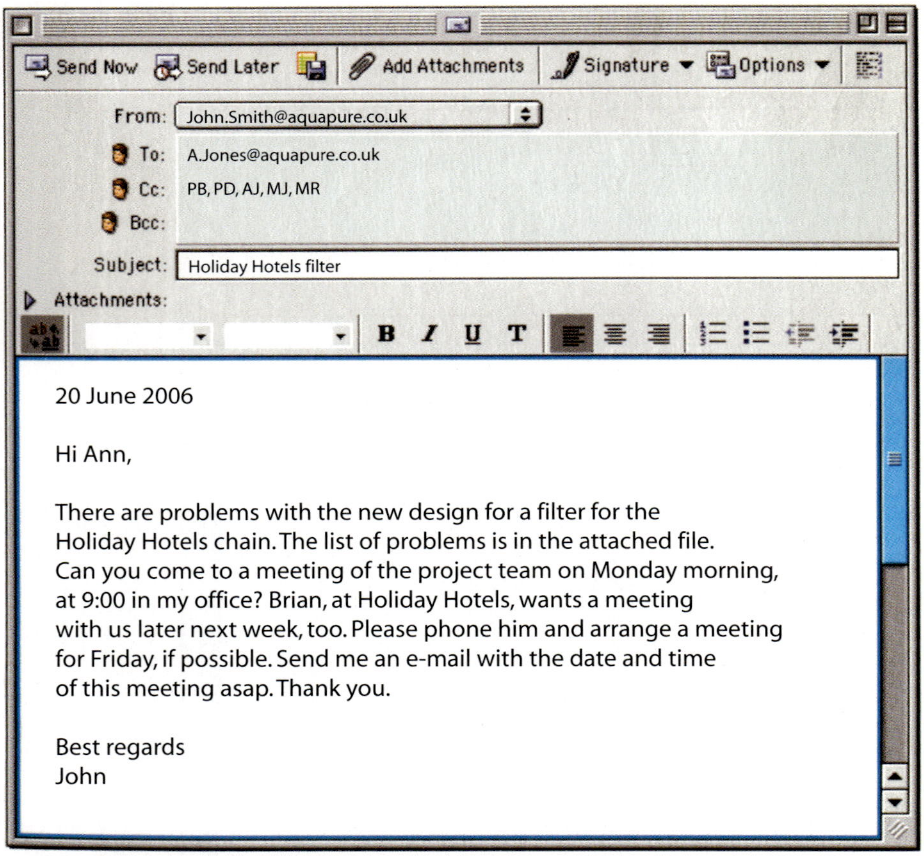

Send Now Send Later Add Attachments Signature Options

From: John.Smith@aquapure.co.uk

To: A.Jones@aquapure.co.uk

Cc: PB, PD, AJ, MJ, MR

Bcc:

Subject: Holiday Hotels filter

Attachments:

20 June 2006

Hi Ann,

There are problems with the new design for a filter for the Holiday Hotels chain. The list of problems is in the attached file. Can you come to a meeting of the project team on Monday morning, at 9:00 in my office? Brian, at Holiday Hotels, wants a meeting with us later next week, too. Please phone him and arrange a meeting for Friday, if possible. Send me an e-mail with the date and time of this meeting asap. Thank you.

Best regards
John

Exercise

22 Right or wrong? Correct the wrong sentences. | **Richtig oder falsch? Korrigieren Sie.**

a) The e-mail is from Ann Jones to John Smith.
b) It is about a meeting with Mr Tailor from the bank.
c) The e-mail is for Ann and ten other colleagues.
d) The list of problems is with the e-mail.
e) The meeting of the project team is next Tuesday at 9:00.
f) It is in Ann's office.
g) Ann must arrange a meeting with John.

23 Find the English for: | **Finden Sie die englischen Entsprechungen für:**

• Anhang • Schicken Sie mir eine E-Mail • wenn möglich

24 Write the following e-mails in English. | **Schreiben Sie die folgenden E-Mails auf Englisch.**

a) Sie schicken eine Namensliste an Tim Thomas als Anhang.
b) Schreiben Sie die E-Mail.
c) Sie schicken Informationen über Produkte als Anhang.
d) Schreiben Sie die Begleit-E-Mail.

Vocabulary Practice

Exercise

25 Match answers in B to expressions in A. | Finden Sie in B eine Antwort zu jedem Satz in A.

A	B
a) What is your name?	(1) I'm fine thanks, and you?
b) Good morning.	(2) Good afternoon.
c) How are you?	(3) She is OK.
d) Goodbye for now.	(4) Pleased to meet you.
e) It's a nice day, isn't it?	(5) Bye. Have a nice day!
f) Good afternoon.	(6) My name is Jane.
g) Pleased to meet you.	(7) Yes, lovely.
h) Where are you from?	(8) Hello.
i) How is Ann?	(9) Germany.

26 Which word doesn't fit? | Welches Wort passt nicht?

- brown • blue • green • hair
- secretary • English teacher • office worker • sales manager
- Leeds • Germany • England • France
- fine • well • bad • OK
- employee • secretary • department • trainee
- good morning • good afternoon • best regards • good evening

Vorsicht:

Boss — Auf Englisch bedeutet das Wort "Chef" so viel wie „Chefkoch/Küchenchef". Wenn Sie also sagen "I want to talk to the chef", dann wird der Koch erscheinen, nicht der Chef! Ihn nennt man auf Englisch "the boss".

Please — "Please" heißt „Bitte", aber "pleased" heißt „erfreut".
"Please" kann man allerdings nicht überall da einsetzen, wo das deutsche „Bitte" passt.
"Please" signalisiert, dass man etwas haben will, z. B. "Please help me!" "Please say your name".

Englisch	Deutsch
"Thank you very much."	„Vielen Dank."
"You are welcome."	„Bitte."

Business Tip

Britische E-Mail-Adressen enden oft mit co.uk
co gibt an, dass es sich um ein Unternehmen handelt und uk bedeutet, dass es eine britische E-Mail-Adresse ist (UK = United Kingdom).

2 Here and now

Speak!

Sie lernen:

aktuelle Tätigkeiten zu beschreiben
(z. B. was man gerade macht),
aktuelle Umstände zu beschreiben
(z. B. die Umgebung),
Fragen mit "who" und "where" zu stellen.

8 Hello, how are you?

Audio Text 8 | Hörtext 8

John Smith is phoning his wife, Emily. She is on holiday at the seaside. He is in his office.

Emily	Hello.
John	Hello, Emily, John here.
Emily	Hi, how are you, John? Are you very busy in the office today? Are you working hard?
John	Yes, I am very busy today. I am preparing for a big meeting. Ann and Paul are writing reports. We are working hard. And you? What are you doing?
Emily	I am sitting on the beach beside the sea. I am sunbathing and reading a magazine. The children are playing. They are making a big sand castle. I wish you were here!
John	I am coming on Friday evening. I'm looking forward to it! Is the sun shining?
Emily	Yes it is. It is hot and the water is warm. The sky is blue. We are having a nice holiday! Susan is learning to swim and Ricky is learning to sail. We are having fun!
John	Good. Give Susan and Ricky my love! See you at the weekend.
Emily	Goodbye, see you soon. Give my regards to Ann and Paul!

Yes,	he/she/it	is.		Yes,	we/they/you	are.
No,	he/she/it	isn't.		No,	we/they/you	aren't.

1 Answer the questions. Use the table above. | Beantworten Sie die Fragen. Benutzen Sie oben stehende Tabelle.

Example/Beispiel

Is John Smith phoning a customer? No, he isn't.

a) Is he at work in his office?
b) Is he phoning his wife, Emily?
c) Is Emily at work today?
d) Is she on holiday with the children?
e) Is John in his office?
f) Are the children at school?
g) Are they playing on the beach?
h) Are they having a nice holiday?
i) Is it raining?
j) Is the sun shining?

2 Answer the questions. | Beantworten Sie die Fragen.

a) What is Susan learning this summer?
b) What is Rickie learning this summer?
c) What are they doing now?
d) Where is John Smith?
e) Where are his wife and children now?
f) Who is Emily?

3 Find the English for: | Finden Sie die englischen Entsprechungen für:

a) Ich freue mich darauf!
b) Wir haben Spaß.
c) Was machst du gerade?
d) Grüß Ann und Paul von mir.

4 Give the short forms and infinitives. | Bilden Sie die Kurzformen und die Stammformen.

a) I am working hard.
b) I am sitting on the beach.
c) He is writing a report.
d) She is working.
e) They are playing on the beach.

Grammar

ing-Form | Verlaufsform

I **am**, he/she/it **is**
we/you/they **are** + Verbstamm + ing = **aktuelle Handlung: das, was jetzt gerade passiert**

I am working.	=	Ich arbeite gerade.
She is sleeping.	=	Sie schläft gerade.
They are coming.	=	Sie kommen gerade.

Rechtschreibung

• work > working • go > going • read > reading • talk > talking • come > coming • make > making • write > writing • phone > phoning • sit > sitting • run > running • stop > stopping

Fragen

• Are you working? • Is he coming? • Is it raining?

Verneinung

• I'm not working. • They are not/(aren't) coming. • It isn't raining.

Kurzantworten

Is he coming? No, he isn't/Yes, he is

Diese Zeitform heißt *Present Progressive* bzw. *Verlaufsform.*
Da es im Deutschen keine entsprechende Zeitform gibt, behilft man sich mit Wörtern wie „gerade" oder „jetzt".

I am learning English. = Ich lerne gerade Englisch.

Exercise

5 Translate into English. | Übersetzen Sie.

a) Ich telefoniere gerade.
b) Wir sprechen gerade.
c) Sie arbeitet jetzt.
d) Der Bus kommt gerade.
e) Wir lesen gerade.
f) Er geht jetzt.
g) Die Kinder lernen Englisch.
h) Ich arbeite gerade nicht.

6 Put in the negative. | Verneinen Sie.

a) I am working today.
b) The sun is shining.
c) My friend is working now.
d) My dog is sleeping.
e) The children are playing.
f) My mother is listening.
g) The secretaries are phoning.
h) The girls are drinking coffee.

This = dieser, diese, dieses hier (wenn ich etwas meine, das sich in meiner Nähe befindet)
That = das da (wenn ich etwas meine, das weiter weg ist)

	Einzahl	Mehrzahl
Nah	this	these
Fern	that	those

Exercise

7 Look at the pictures and answer the questions. | **Beantworten Sie die Fragen.**

Who is this?
Where is he/she?
What is he/she doing?

Example/Beispiel

Who is this?	This is Paul.
Where is he/she?	He is in the office.
What is he/she doing?	He is working at his computer/PC.

8 Make questions. | **Bilden Sie Fragen.**

a) It is raining.
b) He is working.
c) She is eating.
d) We are learning English.
e) They are coming.
f) I am writing a letter.

Die Verlaufsform benutzt man im Englischen, wenn das Geschilderte gerade passiert, z. B. "I am learning English". Wörtlich übersetzt bedeutet das: „Ich bin am Englischlernen"; eine Ausdrucksweise, die im Deutschen höchstens umgangssprachlich möglich ist. Wie so oft, ist auch hier eine wörtliche Übersetzung nicht wünschenswert.

9

Who is that? Where is that?

Audio Text 9 | Hörtext 9

Ann is looking at the photos on Paul's desk, then they are looking at the photos on Ann's desk.

Ann	This is a nice picture, Paul. Who is this, beside you? She is pretty!
Paul	That is my sister, Carla.
Ann	She has blue eyes, like you! And who is this?
Paul	That is my father.
Ann	Here is Carla again. Where is she? And who is that?
Paul	In that photograph, she is in a big park in Berlin. And that is my mother. Carla is with my mother in the park. They are walking with our dog.
Ann	But where is the dog?
Paul	The dog is not in this picture. Here is a picture of our dog. His name is Whisky. He is black and white. And who is this, Ann? Is this your brother?
Ann	No, that is my husband. His name is Tim. He is an English teacher.
Paul	And where is this?
Ann	That is Otley. That is our house in Otley. And these two boys are our sons, Andrew and Harry! Harry has red hair, and Andrew's hair is brown.

Exercise

9 Fill in the gaps. | Füllen Sie die Lücken aus.

a) Paul's sister's name is ______ and his dog is called ______

b) Ann's husband is called ______ and they live in a house in ______

c) Ann is an assistant sales manager and ______ husband is ______ English teacher.

d) Ann and Tim have two sons. Their names are ______ and ______

What is there in Otley?

Audio Text 10 | Hörtext 10

10

Paul — What is Otley like, Ann? Is it big?

Ann — No, it is small. It isn't a town. It is a village, but it is very nice. There are a lot of old houses near the market place. And there is a grey stone church. and a little river with a stone bridge.

Paul — Is there a shop?

Ann — Yes, there is a supermarket.

Paul — Are there any restaurants in Otley?

Ann — No, but there is a pub and there are two cafés. You must come to our house on Sunday. You can have lunch with us, and see an English village.

Paul — Thank you, Ann. That is very kind of you. Is there a railway station in Otley?

Ann — No, but you can take the bus. There are a lot of buses from Leeds to Otley. Here is a bus timetable. There is a bus at 11:00 from Leeds bus station to Otley. It is number 33. There is a bus-stop near our house.

Exercise

10 Answer the questions. | Beantworten Sie die Fragen.

a) Is there a railway station in Otley?
b) Is there a river there?
c) Are there any shops?
d) Are there any cafés?
e) Is there a church?
f) Is there a restaurant?

Grammar

There is no „es gibt" in English | **„Es gibt" gibt es auf Englisch nicht!**

There is a church.	Es gibt eine Kirche.	(There is + Einzahl)
There are two supermarkets.	Es gibt zwei Supermärkte.	(There are + Mehrzahl)
Is there a church?	Gibt es eine Kirche?	
How many shops **are there**?	Wie viele Geschäfte gibt es?	

Exercise

11 Fill in the gaps. | Setzen Sie "is" oder "are" in die Lücken ein.

a) There ______ a church and there ______ a lot of old houses.
b) There ______ two secretaries.
c) There ______ a teacher and there ______ five students.
d) There ______ four pictures on his desk.
e) There ______ a book on my desk.
f) In my town there ______ three churches.
g) In this village there ______ one shop.
h) ______ there a cinema in your town or village?
i) How many shops ______ there in your village?

12 Answer the questions. | Beantworten Sie die Fragen.

a) How many students are there in your class?
b) How many windows are there in your classroom?
c) How many chairs are there?
d) How many tables are there?
e) Is there a clock on the wall?

Now you talk! | Jetzt reden Sie!

1 Questions about now

Ask and answer. | Stellen Sie Fragen und beantworten Sie diese.

What are you doing now?

Are you reading?

What is your friend/mother/father doing now?

Ask more questions. | Stellen Sie einander weitere Fragen.

2 Questions about photos

Bring photos: ask about them. | Bringen Sie Fotos mit und stellen Sie dazu Fragen.

Who is that?/Who are they?

Where is that?

What is he/she doing?/What are they doing?

3 Questions about your home

Talk about your town or village. | Sprechen Sie über Ihre Stadt/Ihr Dorf.

I live in a small/big town/village called ____________

In ____________, there are ____________

and there is a ____________

Word Bank

• university • theatre • sports ground • football stadium • shopping centre
• youth club • disco • concert hall

4 Now work with a partner:

Find out about his/her hometown. | Befragen Sie Ihre/n Partner/in über dessen/deren Wohnort.

5 Learning by playing

In my bag there is/there are ____________

Rules as for „Ich packe meinen Koffer". Regeln wie für „Ich packe meinen Koffer".

"What am I doing?"

Mime an action: the group must say what what it is.

Stellen Sie pantomimisch eine Tätigkeit dar. Die anderen müssen raten, worum es sich handelt.

Phone!

Sie lernen:

Fragen zu stellen,
Telefonnachrichten zu übermitteln.

A call from a friend

11

Audio Text 11 | Hörtext 11

Jane is at home. She isn't working. She is watching TV. Now her mobile phone is ringing.

Jane	Hello.
Susan	Hello, is that Jane?
Jane	Yes, who is that?
Susan	Susan. Susan Townsend.
Jane	Hello Su! How are you? Where are you calling from?
Susan	I'm fine. I'm in Leeds. Are you working? Are you busy?
Jane	No, I'm not busy. I'm watching TV, but it isn't interesting. What are you doing here? Are you staying here long?
Susan	No. I'm on the way to London, but my car is out of order. It stopped on the motorway. A mechanic is repairing it now. I am sitting in the "Hotspot" coffee bar in Market Street. I'm drinking a cappuccino. Can you come here?
Jane	Yes, Market Street is near my flat. I'm coming now. See you in a few minutes.

Exercise

13 Here are some answers. What are the questions? | **Hier sind einige Antworten. Wie lauten die Fragen?**

a) She is at home.
b) Susan Townsend.
c) She is in a coffee-bar in Leeds.
d) No, she isn't. She is on the way to London.
e) Because her car stopped.
f) She is drinking coffee.

A telephone dialogue

12

Listening Comprehension: Audio Text 12 | Hörtext 12

Exercise

14 Listen to Audio Text 12 and complete the message. | **Hören Sie sich Hörtext 12 an und vervollständigen Sie die Mitteilung.**

A telephone message for ______________ taken by ______________

______________ called from ______________

Message: ______________

Write!

Sie lernen:

den Zweck einer E-Mail zu verstehen und darüber zu berichten,
über eine Stadt oder ein Dorf zu berichten.

Exercise

15 Use your dictionary or the word list at the end of the book. Create a list with new words. | **Benutzen Sie Ihr Wörterbuch oder die Wortliste am Ende dieses Buches. Machen Sie eine Liste mit den neuen Vokabeln.**

Dear Mr Smith,

I'm writing about your invoice number 458/ 2007. The invoice is incorrect. The price of the software is £300.00 not £3 000.00. Please send a correct invoice asap.

Best regards,
Margaret Hankin

Dear Ms Hankin,

Thank you for your email about your invoice number 458/ 2007.
I am writing to apologise for the incorrect invoice. I am really very sorry about the mistake. We are sending a correct invoice by letter-post.

Best regards,
John Smith

Dear Mr Smith,

Thanks for your e-mail and the corrected invoice. My bank is transferring three hundred pounds to your company account to pay the invoice.

Kind regards,
Margaret Hankin

16 Write a short report in German: | **Schreiben Sie einen kurzen Bericht auf Deutsch:**

Ms ______ schrieb wegen ______
Sie verlangte eine ______
Mr ______ entschuldigte sich und sagte, dass ______
Ms ______ bedankte sich für ______ und schrieb,
dass ______

Vocabulary Practice

Exercise

17 Which word doesn't fit? | Welches Wort passt nicht?

husband	son	father	mother
supermarket	office	shop	department store
village	chair	table	window
city	company	village	town

18 Sort the words? What goes where? | Sortieren Sie die Wörter. Was gehört wohin?

Office	Town or village	Job	Family

• accountant • bridge • brother • café • chair • church • clock • computer • cousin • desk • director • doctor • engineer • father • grandmother • interpreter • lamp • mother • PC • river • salesman • secretary • translator • window

19 Fill in the missing colour words. | Fügen Sie die entsprechenden Farben ein.

Blue and yellow make ____________

Red and yellow make ____________

The British flag is ____________, ____________ and ____________

The German flag is ____________, ____________ and ____________

20 Find the pairs. | Finden Sie die Wortpaare.

a) I'm sorry	(1) cost
b) incorrect	(2) shop
c) I'll call	(3) wrong
d) price	(4) I'll phone
e) store	(5) I apologise

21 Give the opposite. | Nennen Sie das Gegenteil.

• big • busy • interesting • young • correct

22 Give the English for: | Sagen Sie auf Englisch:

• Rechnung • Abteilung • überweisen • sich entschuldigen

3 Lunch break

Speak!

Sie lernen:

über Preise zu sprechen,
Essen oder Trinken zu bestellen,
über Mengen zu sprechen
(much/many/a lot of).

13 Is it time for lunch?

Audio Text 13 | Hörtext 13

Here is the canteen at Aquapure. What is the time? Look! It is eleven o'clock now. It isn't lunchtime, but the canteen is open. Paul is in the canteen. He is buying a cup of coffee and a cheese roll. He is very hungry and thirsty.

Waitress	Good morning.
Paul	Good morning. Is the canteen open?
Waitress	Yes, it is.
Paul	How much is a cheese roll, please?
Waitress	Two pounds, and a cup of coffee is one pound twenty. That is three pounds and twenty pence.
Paul	Here is a five pound note.
Waitress	Here is your change, one pound and eighty pence. There is milk, and here is sugar.
Paul	Thanks. How much is lunch? Is it expensive?
Waitress	Here is the menu. Look.
Paul	Oh. It is not expensive. It is cheap! When is lunch?
Waitress	Lunch is from twelve o'clock to two o'clock.
Paul	Thanks.
Waitress	You are welcome! See you later!

Exercise

1 Answer the questions. | Beantworten Sie die Fragen.

a) Where is Paul?
b) What is the time?
c) Is the canteen open?
d) Is it lunch time?
e) What is he buying?
f) How much is a cheese roll?
g) How much is a coffee?
h) How much change is there from the five pound note?
i) When is lunch served?

Find out how much one English pound (GBP) is in Euros.
How much is a sandwich and a coffee in Germany? Is it more expensive?

Numbers and Prices

Audio Text 14 | Hörtext 14

14

Exercise

2 Say the numbers one to twenty. | Zählen Sie von eins bis zwanzig.

1 one	2 two	3 three	4 four	5 five
6 six	7 seven	8 eight	9 nine	10 ten
11 eleven	12 twelve	13 thirteen	14 fourteen	15 fifteen
16 sixteen	17 seventeen	18 eighteen	19 nineteen	20 twenty

3 Fill in the missing numbers. | Fügen Sie die fehlenden Zahlen ein.

"Dinner for ______" is a film that many people in Germany watch on New Year's Eve.
"Give me ______" means: give me your hand.
"High noon" is another way of saying ______ o'clock midday.
You can vote when you are ______

LUNCHTIME MENU

Starters

Tomato soup	£2.00
Oxtail soup	£2.00

Main Dishes

Sausage	£3.00
Steak	£4.10
Chicken	£4.20
Fried fish	£4.20

(All served with chips and peas or salad)

Sandwiches or Rolls	£2.00

Desserts

ice cream	£1.50
apple pie	£2.00

TODAY'S SPECIAL

Roast lamb with roast potatoes, peas and mint sauce	£3.50

Drinks

mineral water	£1.10
apple juice	£1.15
coffee	£1.20
tea	£1.00

And you!

Ask and answer questions about the menu. | Stellen Sie und beantworten Sie Fragen zur Speisekarte.

Example/Beispiel

A How much is a tomato soup?

B A tomato soup is two pounds.

Order a meal. | Bestellen Sie ein Essen.

Example/Beispiel

A Sausage please.

B With chips and peas?

A No, with salad, please.

B And to drink?

A Mineral water, please.

B That is four pounds ten, please.

Exercise

4 Count from twenty to one hundred. | Zählen Sie von 20 bis 100.

21 twenty-one	22 twenty-two	27 twenty seven
30 thirty	31 thirty-one	40 forty
50 fifty	55 fifty-five	59 fifty-nine
60 sixty	70 seventy	80 eighty
90 ninety	100 one hundred	103 one hundred and three

5 Read the prices. | Lesen Sie die Preise laut vor.

£10.50	£112.63	£33.75	$20.30
€5.80	€540.00	$10.30	$60.00

6 Answer the questions. | Beantworten Sie die Fragen.

a) How many people are in a football team?
b) How many students are in your English class?
c) How many days are in a week?
d) How many people are in a handball team?
e) How many letters are there in the alphabet?
f) How many keys are there on your mobile phone?
g) How much is a cup of coffee in a German café?
h) How much is a hamburger with chips?
i) How much is a steak and salad?
j) How much money is there in your pocket now?

Grammar

Much/many/a lot of | Viel/viele

Much = viel:	How much time is there? There isn't much bread. There is too much stress.	(Für Dinge, die man nicht zählen kann)
Many = viele:	How many computers are there? There are not many people here. There are too many problems.	(Für Dinge, die man zählen kann)
A lot of = viel *und* viele:	I have a lot of time. There are not a lot of people here.	

In der gesprochenen Sprache benutzt man in bejahten Sätzen eher "a lot of":
"He writes a lot of e-mails."
Much oder *many* sind obligatorisch:
– nach "how": How many people?/How much money?
– nach "too": too many people/too much money.

Exercise

7 Fill the gaps with a lot of, much or many. | Füllen Sie **a lot of, much** oder **many** in die Lücken.

a) How ______ people are in your office?
b) How ______ is a hamburger?
c) There is too ______ sugar in my tea.
d) How ______ milk do you want in your coffee?
e) How ______ money do you have in your bag?
f) How ______ books are there on your desk?
g) I hope you have ______ fun on holiday.

8 "Much" or "many"? | "Much" oder "many"?

a) How ______ milk is there?
b) How ______ cups of coffee is he buying?
c) How ______ potatoes are there?
d) How ______ do the ham sandwiches cost?
e) How ______ water is in the bottle?
f) How ______ problems are there?

Now you talk! | Jetzt reden Sie!

1 And you?

a) How much is a cup of coffee in Germany?
b) How much is a hamburger?
c) How much is a steak with chips?
d) Is there a canteen in your school/office? If yes, how much is lunch there?
e) Look at the menu on page 33. Is the food cheap or expensive?

2 The cafeteria on the Ferryboat has prices in euros.

Work with a partner. | **Arbeiten Sie mit einem Partner.**
A is a customer, B is a waiter/waitress. | **A ist Kunde, B ist Kellner/in.**
Order what you want. | **Bestellen Sie.**

Pot of tea	€3.50	Pot of coffee	€4.00
Cup of tea	€2.00	Espresso	€2.00
Cappuccino	€2.00	Latte	€2.30
Coke	€1.75	Mineral water	€1.50
Crisps	€2.00	Biscuits	€2.30
Sandwich	€4.25	Piece of cake	€2.00

€3.50 = three euros fifty *oder* three euros and fifty cents.

3 Learning by playing

Play "Hufflepuffle" (Für Gruppen ab sechs Personen)
Man zählt bis 400, aber jede Zahl, die eine Drei beinhaltet oder durch drei zu teilen ist, wird ausgelassen. Wer eine „falsche" Zahl sagt, scheidet aus.

Play lottery numbers
Jeder Teilnehmer nennt sechs Zahlen zwischen 1 und 100. Die anderen notieren die Zahlen; wenn Sie Probleme haben, üben Sie weiter!
Der Zweck dieses Spieles ist, herauszufinden wo persönliche Schwierigkeiten beim Verstehen oder Verwenden von Zahlen liegen.

Phone!

Sie lernen:

sich telefonisch nach dem Preis zu erkundigen.

A call to a railway company in England.

Audio Text 15 | Hörtext 15

15

Listen to and read the call. | Hören und lesen Sie den Anruf.

Paul	Hello. Is that Northern Rail?
Employee	Yes, hello. How can I help you?
Paul	How much is a ticket to London from Leeds?
Employee	Single or return?
Paul	Sorry, what? My English is not so good.
Employee	Single is one way. Return is to London and back to Leeds.
Paul	Oh, return, please.
Employee	Day return?
Paul	Pardon? What is that?
Employee	Day return: you go to London and back to Leeds on one day. A day return ticket is only £30.
Paul	No. Weekend, a weekend return.
Employee	There isn't a weekend return. A return ticket to London from Leeds is £45.
Paul	That is expensive!

And you!

Make similar dialogues using the information in the box below. | Bilden Sie mithilfe der folgenden Informationen ähnliche Dialoge.

Journey	day return	return
Leeds to London	£30.00	£45.00
Leeds to Manchester	£15.00	£20.00
Leeds to Loughborough	£20.30	£32.90

Write!

Sie lernen:

Formulare für sich oder andere auszufüllen.

Filling in forms: Formulare ausfüllen

Copy the form and fill it in. | Kopieren Sie das Formular und füllen Sie es aus.

Please use CAPITAL LETTERS and black ink

Family name ____________________ Forename(s) ____________________

Date of birth ____________________ Place of birth ____________________

Nationality ____________________ Occupation ____________________

Marital status (please tick box) married ☐ single ☐ divorced ☐

Address ____
(Please include postal code)

Home phone number ________________________________
Mobile phone number ________________________________
Office phone number ________________________________

Hobbies ____

Signature ____________________ Date ____________

And you!

Now fill in the form for a partner. Find out the information you need. | Jetzt füllen Sie das Formular für eine/n Partner/in aus. Finden Sie die notwendigen Angaben heraus.

Ask: What is your ____________________?
What are your ____________________?
Are you ____________________?

Exercise

Vocabulary Practice

9 Which word doesn't fit and why? | Welches Wort passt nicht? Warum nicht?

lunch	hamburger	breakfast	dinner
starter	main dish	dessert	breakfast
tomato	oxtail	potato	pea
pound	euro	dollar	price
menu	sausage	steak	fish

10 Give the opposite. | Nennen Sie das Gegenteil.

• cheap • hot • later • buy

11 Find the right answer. | Finden Sie die richtige Antwort.

a) Do you want a coffee?	(1) You're welcome.
a) Thank you.	(2) No, thanks, I'll try again later.
b) How are you?	(3) Yes, please.
c) How much is it?	(4) Goodbye.
d) Do you want to hold on?	(5) Two pounds.
e) Here is your change.	(6) Fine, thanks.
f) See you later.	(7) Thanks.

12 Find the right definition. | Finden Sie die richtige Definition.

a) A return ticket	(1) is bread with cheese or meat.
b) A waitress	(2) is not married.
c) An occupation	(3) is a ticket to a place and back.
d) A cappuccino	(4) is English money.
e) A single person	(5) is a job.
f) A sandwich	(6) is a woman-worker in a restaurant or café.
g) A pound	(7) is a cup of coffee with milk on the top.

Speak!

Sie lernen:

über die Zukunft zu sprechen (will/won't),
zu sagen, was man machen kann oder nicht machen kann (can/can't),
Wochentage und Datumsangaben.

16

Arranging a meeting

Audio Text 16 | Hörtext 16

Read and listen to the text. | Lesen und hören Sie den Text.

John Can you come to a team meeting in my office next Monday morning, Pete? It is important. It is about the problems with the design of a new filter for Holiday Hotels.

Peter No, sorry, John. I'm afraid I can't come. I won't be in the office on Monday. I won't be in England. I'll be in Hamburg on a business trip.

John The hotel chain is a big customer. Will you be available later in the week?

Peter Yes, I'll be back on Wednesday evening. We can meet on Thursday morning.

John OK. I'll see you on Thursday, and we'll talk about it. I'll arrange a meeting with the managing director of the Holiday Hotels for Friday. Can you come then?

Peter Yes, I'll be free then. We can discuss the problems on Thursday. Who will be at the team meeting on Monday?

John Well, Ann will be there, and Mary and Steve from the design department, and Mike Richards, the guy from the finance department.

Peter Can you send me a report of the team meeting by e-mail? I can read it in my hotel in Hamburg.

John OK. I'll ask Ann to send you the minutes of the meeting. Have a good trip to Germany, Pete.

Peter Thanks. I'm sure I will. See you on Thursday.

The days of the week.

• Monday • Tuesday • Wednesday • Thursday • Friday • Saturday • Sunday

Exercise

1 Answer the questions. | Beantworten Sie die Fragen.

a) When will the team meet?
b) Where will the meeting be?
c) What will the team talk about?
d) Can Peter go to the meeting?
e) Where will Peter be next Monday?
f) When will he come back to England?
g) Can he read the report of the team meeting before Thursday?
h) Who will John and Peter meet next Friday?

2 Look at the text again. Find the English for: | Sehen Sie sich den Text noch einmal an und übersetzen Sie folgende Sätze:

Es ist wichtig.
Ich bin am Mittwoch zurück.
Ich werde dann frei sein.
(Ich bin) auf Geschäftsreise.
Leider kann ich nicht kommen.
Wir sehen uns am Donnerstag.

3 Answer the questions. | Beantworten Sie die Fragen.

What day is it today?
What day will it be tomorrow?

Business Tip

Vorsicht bei TUESDAY (Dienstag) und THURSDAY (Donnerstag) – hier gerät man leicht durcheinander!
KW = calendar week; aber Vorsicht! Engländer geben oftmals das Datum des betreffenden Montags an und nicht die Kalenderwoche: *The week beginning Monday March 6th* anstatt 10. KW.

Grammar

Can/can't (cannot) | Können/nicht können

I can speak English. = Ich kann Englisch sprechen.
He can't swim. = Er kann nicht schwimmen.
Can they speak Italian? = Können sie Italienisch sprechen?

Will/won't/will not | Werde/werde nicht

I will go/I'll go *(Kurzform)* = Ich werde gehen.
It won't rain = Es wird nicht regnen.

Exercise

Here are some things that Paul Braun can or can't do.

play football	play tennis	speak French	work with a PC	speak English	play the piano
yes (very well)	no	yes (but not very well)	yes	yes (fluently)	no

4 Ask and answer the questions. | Stellen Sie Fragen und beantworten Sie diese.

Example/Beispiel

Can Paul …? Yes, he can/No he can't.

Exercise

5 Put in "will" or "won't". | Setzen Sie "will" oder "won't" ein.

a) I hope it ________ rain tomorrow. I'm having a party.
b) We ________ go to an Italian restaurant for lunch on Tuesday.
c) Next winter it ________ snow.
d) The German football team ________ win the next world cup.

And you!

Ask and answer questions. | Stellen und beantworten Sie Fragen.

Example/Beispiel

Can you play football? Yes, I can/No I can't.

a) Where will you be next Saturday?
b) Will you watch a film tomorrow evening?
c) Will you be at home next week?
d) Will you be at school tomorrow?
e) When will you go on holiday?

17

The company team

Audio Text 17 | Hörtext 17

Read and listen to the text. | Lesen und hören Sie den Text.

John	You can play football well, Paul, can't you?
Paul	Yes, I am good at football. I am in a good team in Germany. But I play soccer, not rugby football.
John	Soccer is our game. Will you play for our company team?
Paul	Yes, of course I will. I'll be happy to play football again.
John	The match with the Holiday Hotels team is next week. Will you play goalkeeper for us?
Paul	When is the match?
John	It is next Saturday.
Paul	I'm afraid I won't be in England then. I can't play for you. I'll be in Germany because it is my mother's birthday next Friday. I will arrive back here on Sunday.
John	That is a pity! But can you come to football training tomorrow evening?
Paul	Yes, I can. I'll see you at the sports ground.

Exercise

6 Answer the questions. | Beantworten Sie die Fragen.

a) Can Paul play football?
b) Will he play for the company team?
c) Where will he be next Saturday?
d) Why can't he play next Saturday?
e) What will he do tomorrow evening?

7 About you! | Nun zu Ihnen!

a) Can you play football?
b) Can you play it well?
c) Can you play goalkeeper?
d) Where will you be next Saturday?
e) Where will you be tomorrow evening?

Grammar

Personal Pronouns | Personalpronomen

Subject		Object	
I	**I** like Peter	me	Peter likes **me**
you	**You** like Peter	you	Peter likes **you**
he	**He** likes Peter	him	Peter likes **him**
she	**She** likes Peter	her	Peter likes **her**
it	**It** likes Peter	it	Peter likes **it**
we	**We** like Peter	us	Peter likes **us**
you	**You** like Peter	you	Peter likes **you**
they	**They** like Peter	them	Peter likes **them**

Exercise

8 Complete. | Ergänzen Sie.

a) Where is my book? Can you see _____?
b) I want to speak to Jane. Please connect me to _____
c) We are coming. Please wait for _____
d) I want that letter. Give it to _____
e) Jane, I am talking to _____. Please listen.
f) The children are hungry. Buy sandwiches for _____
g) Paul is good at football. The office team want _____
h) Jane is pretty. Paul is going to lunch with _____

9 Complete. | Ergänzen Sie.

a) Is Peter here? Can you see _____? Yes, _____ is there, near the window.
b) Carla is my friend. I like _____ _____ is nice.
c) Ann and Paul are in the office. I can see _____
d) Paul is from Germany. _____ is from Berlin.
e) Carla and Jane are not here. _____ are at lunch.

What's the time? | Wie viel Uhr ist es?

Wie im Deutschen, gibt es im Englischen verschiedene Arten, die Uhrzeit zu sagen.

Im Deutschen kann man sagen:
Zehn nach sechs (abends) *oder* sechs Uhr zehn *oder* achtzehn Uhr zehn
Im Englischen kann man sagen:
Ten (minutes) past six (p.m.) *oder* six ten p.m. *oder* eighteen ten

(a) quarter past eight a.m.	eight fifteen
(a) quarter to nine a.m.	eight forty-five
nine o'clock a.m.	nine
half past ten a.m.	ten thirty
two minutes past one p.m.	thirteen two
twelve minutes past one p.m.	thirteen twelve
(a) quarter past six p.m.	eighteen fifteen

Business Tip

Vorsicht: Fehler passieren schnell!
10:30 = (GB) half past ten (wörtlich: halb nach zehn) = (D) halb elf.

Wann benutzt man das Wort "o'clock"?
Das Wort "o'clock" wird nur bei vollen Stunden verwendet. Es ist aber kein Fehler, es wegzulassen.
9:00 = nine o'clock *oder* nine
Falsch: ten past nine o'clock. **Richtig:** ten past nine.

Wann benutzt man "a.m." und "p.m."?
Man benutzt **a.m.** und **p.m.** nur, wenn es sonst nicht klar wäre, ob man z. B. von acht Uhr morgens oder von acht Uhr abends spricht (a.m. = von Mitternacht bis Mittag, p.m. = von Mittag bis Mitternacht).

Exercise

10 What time is it? | Wie viel Uhr ist es?

Bus timetable

Leeds Bus Station	7:20	11:30	13:20	15:00	18:10
Market Street	7:25	11:35	13:25	15:05	18:15
Oldham Road Post Office	7:49	11:59	13:50	15:30	18:40
Otley Bridge	8:10	12:10	14:11	15:45	18:50
Greenham Church	8:30	12:30	14:35	15:55	19:05

And you!

Say a time. Ask when is the next bus to Otley. | **Nennen Sie eine Zeit. Fragen Sie nach dem nächsten Bus nach Otley.**

Example/Beispiel

A It is now eight o'clock. When is the next bus to Otley?
B At ten past eight.
A Thank you.

Monday Morning

Audio Text 18 | Hörtext 18

18

Read and listen to the text. | Lesen und hören Sie den Text.

Paul	Hi Jane. What's the time?
Jane	Good morning, Paul. It is past nine o'clock. Look! There is the clock!
Paul	Oh no! I'm late again. I'll be late for the meeting! It starts at 9:00. I must hurry. But Jane, can we meet for lunch at 12:15 today?
Jane	No, sorry Paul, I can't. Not today. I can't go out to lunch today. I am alone here at reception.
Paul	And tomorrow. Can you have lunch with me tomorrow?
Jane	OK. At what time?
Paul	At 12:00. I'll meet you here. OK? And we can go to a nice restaurant.
Jane	Thanks, Paul. See you then!
Paul	Now I really must hurry! See you tomorrow.

11 Answer the questions. | Beantworten Sie die Fragen.

Exercise

a) Look at the picture. What is the time?
b) Is the meeting at 10:00 o'clock?
c) Is Paul late for the meeting?
d) Can Jane have lunch with Paul today?
e) Why not?
f) Can she have lunch with him tomorrow?
g) When will they meet?
h) Where will they meet?
i) Where will they go for lunch?

A date for lunch

Audio Text 19 | Hörtext 19

19

Jane	Hi, Ann. Where is Paul? It is 12:14 now. He is late for our date.
Ann	Paul is always late! But look, he is coming now!
Jane	Good! I am hungry!
Paul	Hi Ann. Hello Jane. Sorry I'm late. I am very busy today!
Jane	Hello Paul. Nice to see you, but you are late! Are you hungry too, Ann?
Ann	No, thank you. I'm not hungry. Have a nice lunch! Cheerio for now.
Paul	See you soon, Ann. Come on, Jane. Let's go!

Exercise

12 Now ask the questions! | **Jetzt stellen Sie die Fragen!**

a) It is 12:10 now. — What ____________
b) Paul is late. — Who ____________
c) Jane is hungry. — Who ____________
d) No, she isn't. — Is Ann ____________

13 Find the English for: | **Suchen Sie im Text die englische Entsprechung für:**

• Er kommt immer zu spät. • Er kommt gerade. • Ich habe Hunger. • Schön, dich zu sehen. • Tschüss, bis später. • Gehen wir.

14 Here are some answers – ask the questions. | **Hier ein paar Antworten – stellen Sie die Fragen.**

a) No, I can't play tennis.
b) Yes, I'll be at home this evening.
c) No, sorry, I can't go to the cinema with you.
d) The report will be finished tomorrow.
e) In Berlin? I'll be there on Friday.
f) No, I won't be here at the weekend.

Now you talk! | Jetzt reden Sie!

And you!

Find out what your partner can do. | Finden Sie heraus, was Ihr/e Partner/in alles kann.

Example/Beispiel

Can you type? Yes, I can. I can type very well.
Yes, I can, but not very well.
I can, but only a little bit.
No, I can't.

Word Bank

• type • speak French • dance • play the piano • ride a horse • ski • speak English • cook • sing • play tennis

1 Ask and answer about the future. | Stellen Sie Fragen, die sich auf die Zukunft beziehen und beantworten Sie diese.

a) Where will you be next summer?
b) Will it be sunny tomorrow?
c) Which German football team will be the best this year?
d) Which actors and actresses will get Oscars?
e) What will you do next weekend?
f) At what time will you get up tomorrow?
g) When will you take your next holiday?
h) What time will you get home today?
i) What time will you leave home tomorrow?

2 Ask and answer about about times. | Stellen Sie Fragen zur Zeit und beantworten Sie diese.

a) When is your lunch break?
b) When is breakfast time?
c) What is the time now?
d) What is the time in New York now?
e) When is the end of this lesson?
f) When is the first lesson every day?

Phone!

Sie lernen:

Telefonnummern zu erfragen und weiterzugeben.

20

Please give me your number.

Audio Text 20 | Hörtext 20

Ann Please give me your number.
Caller 0049 64341210.
Ann Sorry, can you repeat that?
Caller 0049, that is the dialling code for Germany, then 64341210.
Ann Thanks. John will call you back.
Caller That is my office number. After six o'clock in the evening, he must call my mobile phone number. It is 0049 6213 893.
Ann 0049 6213 893. Is that correct?
Caller Yes, that is right. But only in the evenings, please. I will try to ring John again after lunch. Please give me his extension number.
Ann Yes, of course, you can dial him direct on 0044 1987 4323832.
Caller Thank you.

Exercise

15 Match the English and German terms. | Ordnen Sie die passenden Begriffe zu.

dialling code	Durchwahl
mobile phone number	Vorwahl
ring	wählen
extension number	Handynummer
dial	anrufen

Business Tip

Nennen Sie bei Telefonnummern immer einzelne Zahlen:
06434 5670: oh six four three four five six seven oh
oder: zero six four three four five six seven zero

Null = OH (britisch) oder ZERO (amerikanisch)

0044 (dialling code for GB) = oh oh four four oder double oh double four
oder zero zero four four oder double zero double four.

Handy heißt auf Englisch übrigens "mobile phone" oder kurz "mobile"!

Read the telephone numbers aloud. | Lesen Sie die Telefonnummern laut vor.

• 04323 234 92 • 0033 5623 8877 • 0172 6969689 • 08834

Can I speak to Joan Miller?

Audio Text 21 | Hörtext 21

21

Assistant	Hello. Smith's Ltd, Tony speaking.
Ann	Hello. This is Ann Jones from Aquapure Ltd. Can I speak to Joan Miller, please?
Assistant	Sorry, Joan is not available. She is in a meeting. I am her assistant. Can I help you?
Ann	I must talk to Joan. When can I reach her?
Assistant	She won't be in today. She will be in tomorrow. Can I give her a message?
Ann	Yes, please. Say she must phone me as soon as possible.
Assistant	OK, Ann. Please give me your telephone number.
Ann	Joan has my office number. My mobile number is 061 654 234.
Assistant	061 654 234. Is that correct?
Ann	Yes, that's right.
Assistant	OK. I will give Joan your message.
Ann	Thanks. Bye.
Assistant	Goodbye, have a nice day.

Exercise

16 Write the phone message for Joan Miller. | Schreiben Sie die Nachricht für Joan Miller auf.

17 Find the English for: | Suchen Sie im Text die englischen Begriffe für:

a) Sie ist heute Morgen nicht erreichbar.
b) Wann kann ich sie erreichen?
c) Ich gebe Ihnen meine Handynummer.
d) Sie hat meine Geschäftsnummer.
e) Kann ich ihr etwas ausrichten?
f) Geben Sie mir bitte Ihre Nummer.
g) Ist das richtig?

18 Translate into English. | Übersetzen Sie ins Englische.

a) Bitte sagen Sie mir Ihre Telefonnummer.
b) Kann ich bitte Herrn Thomas sprechen?
c) Tut mir leid, er ist nicht erreichbar.
d) Wann kann ich ihn erreichen?
e) Kann ich ihm etwas ausrichten?

22

What is your phone number?

Listening Comprehension: Audio Text 22 | Hörtext 22

Listen and write down the six telephone numbers. | **Hören Sie zu und schreiben Sie die sechs Telefonnummern auf.**

1. ______
2. ______
3. ______
4. ______
5. ______
6. ______

And you!

a) Find out your partner's home telephone number, mobile number, office phone number.
b) Write the numbers down.
c) Check that your partner has written your numbers correctly.

Erfragen Sie die Privatnummer, die Handynummer und die Büronummer Ihres Partners.
Schreiben Sie sich die Nummern auf.
Überprüfen Sie, ob Ihr Partner die Telefonnummern korrekt aufgeschrieben hat.

23

Another phone call

Listening Comprehension: Audio Text 23 | Hörtext 23

Listen to Audio Text 23 and answer the following questions. | **Hören Sie sich Hörtext 23 an und beantworten Sie die folgenden Fragen.**

a) What is Jane's phone number?
b) Is it her mobile number?
c) What is Paul's number?
d) Is it his mobile number?
e) When is Paul usually at home in the evening?
f) When will he be at home this evening?

Write!

Sie lernen:

eine informelle Besprechung per E-Mail zu arrangieren.

An invitation to a meeting

Read the e-mails and answer the questions below. Do not translate the mails.

Lesen Sie die E-Mails und beantworten Sie die Fragen. Keine Übersetzung!

Dear team member,

There will be a meeting of the software project team at 11:00 next Monday in room 342. Please confirm that you can come. The agenda is in the attached file.

Best regards
John Smith

Hi John!

I will be at the software project team meeting on Mon. June 7th. Thank you for the agenda.

Best regards
Mike

Dear John,

Sorry, I will not be at the meeting next Monday. I will be on holiday then.

Best regards
Mary

Dear John,

Thank you for the invitation to the team meeting on Monday. I will come to the meeting, but I will be a little bit late, because I must meet a customer at 10:00.

Best regards
Steve

Exercise

19 Answer the questions. | Beantworten Sie die Fragen.

a) Who is arranging the team meeting?
b) When will the meeting be?
c) Where will it be?
d) Who can come?
e) Who can't come?
f) Who will come late?

20 Find the English for: | Suchen Sie die englischen Entsprechungen für:

a) Bestätigen Sie bitte, dass Sie kommen können.
b) Danke für die Einladung.
c) Die Tagesordnung befindet sich im Anhang.
d) Ich werde etwas später kommen.

Travel arrangements

Dear Ann,

I will arrive at London Heathrow airport at 14:45 on Monday June 15th on flight BA 843. Please confirm that you can collect me at the airport.

Kind regards,
Margret Braun

Hi Margret,

I will be at Heathrow at two forty-five on Monday June 15th.
I look forward to seeing you again.

Best wishes,
Ann

Exercise

21 Read the e-mails and answer the questions below. | Lesen Sie die E-Mails und beantworten Sie die Fragen.

a) Who will arrive at Heathrow on Monday?
b) On what date?
c) What is the flight number?
d) Who will meet her at the airport?

22 Give the English for: | Übersetzen Sie ins Englische:

Ich komme um 15:00 in London Heathrow an.
Ich freue mich darauf, Sie wiederzusehen.

23 Write appropriate texts in English. | Schreiben Sie entsprechende E-Mail Texte auf Englisch.

a) Sie laden mehrere Kollegen zu einer Besprechung in Raum 189 um 10:00 Uhr am Montag, den 8. Juni ein.
b) Sie laden einen Freund/eine Freundin zu Ihrer Party am nächsten Samstag ein.

Vocabulary Practice

Exercise

24 Which day is it? | Um welchen Tag handelt es sich?

a) The first day of the week:
b) The day before the week-end:
c) A day when office workers are not at work, but shop assistants are:
d) The day between Monday and Wednesday:
e) If today is Wednesday, what day is it tomorrow?
f) TGIF stands for: Thank God it's
g) The day when most people in Germany and England do not go to work:

25 Find the pairs with the same meaning. | Finden Sie die Wortpaare mit gleicher Bedeutung.

a) I'm afraid.	(1) arrange (a meeting)
b) I'll be available.	(2) come
c) talk about	(3) pleased
d) arrive	(4) cheerio
e) report (of a meeting)	(5) minutes (of a meeting)
f) organise (a meeting)	(6) I'll be free.
g) happy	(7) discuss
h) goodbye	(8) I'm sorry.

26 What games can you play? | Welche Spiele kennen Sie?

Write a list of games in English. How many are the same in German?

27 Put the meals in the right order. | Bringen Sie die Mahlzeiten in die richtige Reihenfolge.

• dinner • breakfast • coffee break • tea • lunch

28 Give the English for: | Übersetzen Sie ins Englische:

a) Bitte bestätigen Sie, dass Sie kommen können.
b) Ich komme um 10:00 Uhr an.
c) Die Flugnummer ist LH 213.
d) Danke für die Einladung.

Speak!

Sie lernen:

Anweisungen zu erteilen,
Wegbeschreibungen zu geben,
höflich um etwas zu bitten.

24

A problem at work!

Audio Text 24 | Hörtext 24

Read and listen to the text. | Lesen und hören Sie den Text.

Ann	Hi, Paul. What is the problem?
Paul	The copier is out of order! Look. The green light isn't on.
Ann	Oh dear! We must tell John! He wants the copies of the report now. No, wait a moment. Look, Paul, the plug of the copying machine isn't in the socket! Put the plug in the socket.
Paul	Yes, you are right. I will plug it in. Oh. It is still out of order!
Ann	Switch the machine on, Paul. Press the switch, there, on the left. Now the light is on. No, don't press the black button now. Wait. Look, the copier has a message: "Warming up; please wait"
John	*(from the office)* Paul, where are you! Please hurry. Bring me the copies of the report. Ann, please come here! Please find Mr Clark's ad-dress and send him a copy. And we must send copies to six people. Look at this list and print the addresses on the envelopes. And write a letter to send with the reports.
Ann	Please make ten copies, Paul. Don't wait for the copier to finish! Come and help me. You can come back and get the copies in five minutes!

Exercise

1 Correct the incorrect statements. | Korrigieren Sie die falschen Aussagen.

a) The copier is out of order.
b) The plug is not in the socket.
c) The copier is switched on.
d) John is not in the office.
e) Paul must make two copies of the report.
f) He must wait until the copies are finished.
g) Ann must send copies to seven people.

Grammar

Instructions and requests | **Anweisungen und Bitten**

Press the button.	Drücken Sie auf den Knopf/Drück auf den Knopf/Drückt auf den Knopf.
Don't press the button.	Nicht auf den Knopf drücken! Drücken Sie nicht auf den Knopf! Drückt/Drück nicht auf den Knopf!

Es hört sich gleich viel höflicher an, wenn man "please" hinzufügt:
Please come/Please don't go. Open the door, please.

Exercise

2 Find the English in the text for: | Suchen Sie folgende englische Sätze im Hörtext.

a) Stecken Sie den Stecker in die Steckdose.
b) Schalten Sie die Maschine an.
c) Warten Sie einen Moment.
d) Drücken Sie nicht auf den schwarzen Knopf.
e) Warten Sie nicht auf die Kopien.
f) Schreiben Sie einen Brief.
g) Bitte kommen Sie hierher.

3 Give the instructions in English. | Erteilen Sie die Anweisungen auf Englisch.

a) Öffnen Sie den Brief nicht.
b) Schicken Sie eine E-Mail.
c) Öffnen Sie nicht den Anhang.
d) Bitte warten Sie fünf Minuten.
e) Bitte sagen Sie mir Ihren Namen.
f) Bitte geben Sie mir Ihre Telefonnummer.
g) Kommen Sie zu der Besprechung.
h) Spielen Sie nicht Fußball.

Please tell me the way

Audio Text 25 | Hörtext 25

25

John	Paul, take these envelopes to the Post Office now. Hurry, please! Take this ten-pound note. Don't forget to ask for a receipt.
Paul	OK. But ...
John	Hurry up, Paul. Don't stand there. The post will go before you get there.
Paul	Excuse me, Jane, can you tell me the way to the Post Office, please?
Jane	The Post Office in Edmont Street? Yes, go out of the door and turn right. Walk down Oldham Road, and take the second turning on the left. At the traffic-lights, cross the road and go straight ahead. Then you will see it, on the right, next to the supermarket.
Paul	Thanks, Jane. See you soon.
Jane	Goodbye for now!

Exercise

4 Find the English for: | **Finden Sie die englischen Entsprechungen.**

a) An der Ampel überqueren Sie die Straße.
b) Wie komme ich zur Post?
c) Biegen Sie rechts ab.
d) Gehen Sie die Oldham Road entlang.
e) Gehen Sie geradeaus.
f) Nehmen Sie die zweite Straße links.

Excuse me heißt zwar „Entschuldigung", aber nur, wenn man jemanden auf sich aufmerksam machen will, zum Beispiel, wenn man eine Frage hat. Wenn man etwas gemacht hat, wofür man sich entschuldigen möchte, zum Beispiel, wenn man jemanden auf den Fuß getreten hat, sagt man "sorry", nicht "excuse me".

Word Bank

- Go straight on. • Go to the main road, then turn left. • Follow the main road.
- Go past the church. • Go over the railway bridge. • Turn right at the cross-roads.
- Take the second turning on the right. • It is on the left.

And you!

Use the plan above: ask the way and tell the way. | Benutzen Sie den oben abgebildeten Plan. Fragen Sie nach dem Weg und beschreiben Sie ihn.

Example/Beispiel

Excuse me, can you tell me the way to the cinema? Yes, of course.

A busy morning at reception

Audio Text 26 | Hörtext 26

Read and listen to the text. | Lesen und hören Sie den Text.

26

Dialogue 1

Jane	Good morning. Can I help you?
Brian Clark	Yes, I have an appointment with Mr Smith. For this morning.
Jane	One moment, please. I'll phone him and tell him you are here. Please tell me your name.
Brian	Clark, Brian Clark, from Holiday Hotels. I am the managing director.
Jane	*(on the phone)* Hello John. Mr Clark is here to see you. From Holiday Hotels. OK, Mr Clark. Someone is coming to meet you. Please wait here. Please take a seat.
Ann	Good morning Brian. Please come this way. I'm Ann Jones. We have often talked on the phone.

Dialogue 2

Jane	Good morning. Can I help you?
Electrician	Yes, I'm from the electricity company. There is a problem in the finance department. Can you tell me the way there?
Jane	Yes, of course. Please show me your company identification card.
Electrician	Here.
Jane	Thanks. Take the lift to the second floor. Then turn right. Go to room 214. That is Mr Green's office. He is the finance manager. He will be happy to see you!

Dialogue 3

Jane	Hi, Paul. Are you late again?
Paul	Oh dear! Is it really 9:15?
Jane	Yes. Don't stand here talking! Hurry! The meeting is starting!
Paul	Bye, Jane. See you soon.

5 Answer the following questions. | Beantworten Sie die folgenden Fragen.

Exercise

a) Who is Mr Clark?
b) Where is he now?
c) He has an appointment. Who with?
d) Where is there a problem in the electricity supply?
e) Who is the finance manager?
f) Where is his office?
g) Who is late for a meeting?

Now you talk! | Jetzt reden Sie!

1 The way

Ask the way and tell the way. | **Fragen Sie nach dem Weg, erklären Sie den Weg.**

Please tell me/us the way from here to your house.
to a restaurant.
to a supermarket.
to the post office.
to the railway station.

2 Learning by playing.

Where am I now? | **Wo bin ich jetzt?**

Jemand beschreibt den Weg von dem Punkt, wo Sie sich alle befinden, zu einem anderen, allgemein bekannten Ort. Die Zuhörer müssen herausfinden, welcher Ort gemeint ist.

Word Bank

• traffic lights	Ampel	• zebra crossing	Zebrastreifen
• turning	Abzweigung	• drive	fahren
• on the left	links	• take bus number 2	nehmen Sie Bus Linie 2
• opposite	gegenüber	• cross roads	Kreuzung
• next to	neben	• second	zweite
• cross (the road)	(die Straße) überqueren	straight on	geradeaus
• turn	abbiegen	• roundabout	Kreisverkehr
• first	erste	• walk	gehen
• on the right	rechts		

And you!

Tell your partner: | **Sagen Sie Ihrem Partner:**

– how to use the copying machine
– how to use a PC
– how to use your mobile phone

Phone!

Sie lernen:

auf Englisch zu buchstabieren,
Namen und E-Mail-Adressen zu notieren.

A call from Germany

Audio Text 27 | Hörtext 27

27

Jane	Hello, Aquapure Ltd. How can I help you?
Caller	Please connect me to Mr Smith.
Jane	One moment please. Sorry, he is not available.
Caller	Please can you give him a message?
Jane	Yes, of course. Please tell me your name.
Caller	Meier. Siegfried Meier. I'm calling from Hamburg.
Jane	Please spell your family name.
Caller	M-E-I-E-R.
Jane	Thanks, Mr Meier. Oh, please tell me your number.
Caller	0049 5430 234.
Jane	Please repeat that.
Caller	0049, for Germany, then 5430 234. I'll give you my e-mail address, too. It's s.meier@t-com.de.
Jane	"at T minus com dot D E." Is that correct?
Caller	Yes, that is right.
Jane	And what is the message?
Caller	Please ask him to call me.
Jane	Ok. I'll give him the message. Goodbye!
Caller	Thanks. Goodbye.

Exercise

6 Correct the incorrect statements. | Berichtigen Sie die falschen Aussagen.

a) Mr Meier wants to talk to Jane.
b) Mr Smith is in his office.
c) The caller's name is Smith.
d) The caller is calling from London.

7 Find the English for: | Suchen Sie im Hörtext 27 die entsprechenden englischen Sätze:

a) Bitte buchstabieren Sie Ihren Familiennamen.
b) Bitte wiederholen Sie das.
c) Bitte sagen Sie mir Ihre Telefonnummer.
d) Können Sie ihm etwas ausrichten?
e) Sagen Sie ihm, er soll mich anrufen.

28

Can you spell in English? Können Sie auf Englisch buchstabieren?

Audio Text 28 | Hörtext 28

Letter	Sounds like		Name code		International code
A	eh	for	Andrew		Alpha
B	bie	for	Benjamin		Bravo
C	ssie	for	Charlie		Charlie
D	die	for	David		Delta
E	ie	for	Edward		Echo
F	eff	for	Freddie		Foxtrot
G	djie	for	George		Golf
H	ehtsch	for	Harry		Hotel
I	ei	for	Isabel		India
J	djeh	for	Jack		Juliett
K	keh	for	Katie		Kilo
L	ell	for	Lucy		Lima
M	emm	for	Mary		Mike
N	enn	for	Nellie		November
O	oh	for	Oliver		Oscar
P	pie	for	Peter		Papa
Q	kyou	for	Queenie		Quebec
R	ah	for	Richard		Romeo
S	ess	for	Susan		Sierra
T	tie	for	Thomas		Tango
U	you	for	Ursula		Uniform
V	wie	for	Victor		Victor
W	dabbelyou	for	William		Whiskey
X	ächs	for	X-ray		X-Ray
Y	why	for	Young		Yankee
Z	zed	for	Zoë		Zulu

Some useful expressions:

• / slash • _ underscore • <u>underline</u> • . dot • @ at • ( ) brackets • - dash
• " " inverted commas • *italics* • **bold** • CAPITAL LETTERS

Business Tip

Vorsicht bei: A, I, E, R, V und W!
Benutzen Sie den Code (z. B. Alfa, Bravo usw.) NUR, wenn Missverständnisse vermieden werden sollen! Sagen Sie aber nie nur das Wort, sondern nennen Sie zuerst den Buchstaben: "A for Alpha" oder "A for Andrew". Im Englischen gibt es keine Umlaute; Ä, Ö und Ü werden AE, OE bzw. UE buchstabiert.

Für E-Mail-Adressen braucht man:

• @ at • . dot • / slash • – minus • \ back-slash

Can you take messages?

Listening Comprehension: Audio Text 29 | Hörtext 29

Listen to Audio Text 29 and write the words or addresses. | **Hören Sie Hörtext 29 an und schreiben Sie die Wörter oder Adressen auf.**

1. ______________________________
2. ______________________________
3. ______________________________
4. ______________________________

And you!

Tell your partner your e-mail address. | **Sagen Sie Ihrem Partner Ihre E-Mail-Adresse.**
Check that he/she has it right.

Can you read it correctly?

Audio Text 30 | Hörtext 30

Read the following sentences aloud, then listen to Audio Text 30. | **Lesen Sie die Sätze, hören Sie sich danach Hörtext 30 an.**

1. His name is Grünermeyer: You spell that G:R:U:E:N:E:R:M:E:Y:E:R.
2. You spell it W:O:R:C.E:S:T:E:R, but you say Worcester sauce!
3. Her e-mail address is rene.lalland@wanadoo.fr.
4. Please send me article number FRA/23.
5. The number of the car is AT RI 312
6. You spell it R:I:G:H:T and not W:R:I:T:E.
7. The correct postal code is IPS 21 ZP
8. The name of the town is Bad Camberg. You spell that capital B: small A:D: new word capital C then small A:M:B:E:R:G.
9. The name of the company is Schmidt GmbH. You spell that S:C:H:M:I:D:T.
10. His car is a VW, not a BMW.

Exercise

8 Translate into English. | Übersetzen Sie ins Englische.

a) Bitte buchstabieren Sie Ihren Namen.
b) Sagen Sie es noch mal.
c) Die Artikelnummer ist AVR/26.
d) Sagen Sie mir bitte seine Autonummer.
e) Ist das ein neues Wort?
f) Können Sie das Wort bitte buchstabieren?
g) Ist das richtig?

31

Business calls?

Audio Text 31 | Hörtext 31

Dialogue 1

John	This is John Smith speaking. Can I speak to Siegfried, please?
Sekretärin	Ja, natürlich. Ich stelle durch. Tut mir leid, er spricht gerade. Wollen Sie warten?
John	Yes, I'll hold on.
Sekretärin	Die Leitung ist frei. Ich verbinde.
Siegfried	Guten Tag, John. Danke für den Anruf.
John	Hello, Siegfried. Thanks for your message. How can I help you?
Siegfried	Wie heißt diese Frau, die mit uns in Berlin war? Sie kommt aus London.
John	Her name is Eva Smythe.
Siegfried	Wie schreibt man Smythe?
John	S:M:Y:T:H:E.

Dialogue 2

Jane	Hello.
Paul	Hallo. Bist du das, Jane?
Jane	Yes, who is that?
Paul	Paul am Apparat. Wie geht es dir, Jane?
Jane	Fine, thanks. Where are you?
Paul	Ich bin zu Hause. Können wir uns heute Abend treffen?
Jane	Yes, OK. At the disco "Saturnalia", at about 10:30.
Paul	Welche Disko? Kannst du das bitte buchstabieren?
Jane	OK. S:A:T:U:R:N:A:L:I:A.
Paul	Wo ist das?
Jane	In Leicester Road. Number 126.
Paul	Okay. Bis bald.

Exercise

9 Translate the German sentences into English, then listen to Audio Text 31 and compare.

Übersetzen Sie die deutschen Sätze ins Englische und vergleichen Sie anschließend mit Hörtext 31.

Write!

Sie lernen:

das Datum auf Englisch
korrekt zu schreiben und zu lesen,
eine Einladung zu schreiben.

Writing the date. | Das Datum schreiben.

Bei 1, 2, 3 muss man aufpassen: 1st = first, 21st = twenty-first, 31st = thirty-first
2nd = second, 22nd = twenty-second
3rd = third, 23rd = twenty-third.

An alle anderen Zahlen hängt man einfach th, z. B. 4th, 5th, 6th usw. bis zu 29th und 30th.

Monate werden großgeschrieben:
2nd May, 4th July, 8th December, May 2nd, July 4th, December 8th.
Die Monatsnamen kann man folgendermaßen abkürzen: Jan., Feb., Mar., Apr. etc.

Months

Listening Comprehension: Audio Text 32 | Hörtext 32

32

Exercise

10 Put the months in the correct order. Listen to Audio Text 32 and compare. | Ordnen Sie die Monate. Hören Sie Hörtext 32 und vergleichen Sie.

• July • January • October • June • September • May • February • August • March • December • April • November

11 Why not write an all-figure date? | Warum das Datum nicht in Ziffern schreiben?
Natürlich kann man das Datum auch so schreiben: 06.09.2007. Aber es gibt ein Problem: US-Amerikaner schreiben 09/06/2007 für den sechsten September (September 6th); Engländer hingegen schreiben 06.09.2007 für den sechsten September. Der 09.06.2009 bezeichnet für Engländer also den neunten Juni (= June 9th)! Um mögliche Missverständnisse zu vermeiden, schreiben Sie das Datum lieber alphabetisch!

12 Write. | Schreiben Sie.

Today's date
Tomorrow's date
Your birthday
Your mother's birthday

13 Answer the following questions. | Beantworten Sie die folgenden Fragen.
When is Mother's Day?
When is the next public holiday in Germany?
When is Halloween?

Exercise

Special days and public holidays

14 Fit a date to a day. | Finden Sie für jeden Tag das passende Datum.

25th December	New Year's day
1st January	Christmas eve
1st May	Valentine's day
4th July	Labour day
24th December	Christmas day
31st December	Independence day
14th February	New Year's eve

Which days are not public holidays in Germany?
Which day is a special public holiday in the USA but nowhere else?

15 A rhyme about the months of the year. | Fügen Sie die fehlenden Zahlen ein.

• 28 • 29 • 30 • 31

______ days are in September,
April, June and November.
The others all have ______
But February, all alone
has ______ days in a normal year
and ______ when it's leap year. (leap year = Schaltjahr)

And you!

Make a calendar for next week. Write in two or more appointments for each day. | Erstellen Sie einen Kalender für die nächste Woche. Fügen Sie zwei (oder mehr) Termine für jeden Tag ein.

Example/Beispiel

Monday 8:00 – 12:30 = school, Monday evening 7:00 = Fitness centre.
Tuesday 10:00 = doctor, Tuesday 13:00 = Lunch with Tim.

Now organise a meeting with your partner. Find a time when you are both free. | Organisieren Sie jetzt ein Treffen mit Ihrem Partner. Finden Sie einen Termin, an dem Sie beide Zeit haben.

Business Tip

Wenn Sie mit Geschäftspartnern, die außerhalb Deutschlands tätig sind, telefonieren und keine Antwort bekommen, prüfen Sie, ob dort nicht vielleicht gerade Feiertag ist. Wenn Sie am 4. Juli in New York anrufen, wird niemand im Büro sein!

Reading or saying the date: | **Das Datum lesen oder sagen:**

Das Datum wird unterschiedlich ausgesprochen und geschrieben:

July 1st	= **the** first **of** July	oder	July **the** first
May 2nd	= **the** second **of** May	oder	May **the** second
12 September	= **the** twelfth **of** September	oder	September **the** twelfth

The Year	**Das Jahr**
1784	= seventeen eighty-four
1999	= nineteen ninety-nine
2000	= two thousand
2001	= two thousand and one

Exercise

16 Read the following dates. | **Lesen Sie folgende Daten.**

- 31.01.1999 • 17.12.2004 • 07.03.2008 • 11.04.2009
- 09/11/2001 • 12/25/2004 • 05/08/2006 • 07/22/2010

17 Read the invitation below and answer the questions. | **Lesen Sie die unten stehende Einladung und beantworten Sie die Fragen.**

When and where is the party?
How much is a ticket to the party?
Who is this invitation from?

18 Write an invitation to a party. | **Schreiben Sie eine Einladung zu einer Party.**

An invitation to an office party

Hi, colleagues.
There will be an office Christmas party on Friday, December 4th at the Holiday Hotel, Leeds, from 19:00 to 24:00. There will be a free dinner, and a disco. (You must pay for your drinks).
I hope you can all come! Please let me know by return e-mail.
Best wishes
Jane

Exercise

Vocabulary Practice

Prepositions: at, in, on | Präpositionen

Wenn es um Zeit geht:

on + Tag	on Monday, on Friday evening, on May 3rd
in + Monat oder Jahreszeit	in April, in Spring
in + Jahr	in 2004
at + Uhrzeit	at 10:00 o'clock
at + Feier	at Christmas (aber **on** Christmas day)
at + the weekend	at the weekend

19 Complete: | Ergänzen Sie.

a) He will come to England ______ Christmas.
b) I was born ______ 1984.
c) There will be more flowers ______ April.
d) The meeting is ______ 9:00.
e) You can go skiing ______ winter.
f) Please phone me ______ the evening.

20 Put in the right order. | Bringen Sie die folgenden Zeitangaben in die richtige Reihenfolge.

• today • yesterday • last week • tomorrow • next week • this morning

Vorsicht:

Date	= Datum	The date today is April 22nd.
Date	= Rendezvous	I have a date with my boy-friend.
Appointment	= Termin	Mr Smith has an appointment with the bank manager.
Data	= Daten (am PC)	Save the data before you close the program.

6 Small talk

Speak!

Sie lernen:

über Gewohnheiten und tägliche Aktivitäten zu erzählen oder Fragen zu stellen (Simple Present 1).

What do you like?

Audio Text 33 | Hörtext 33

33

Paul	Do you like football, Jane?
Jane	No, I don't. I hate football! I'm sorry Paul. You like it, don't you?
Paul	Yes, I do. But never mind! What about music. You like music, don't you?
Jane	Yes, I like music. I like "Angel Singers" a lot.
Paul	Oh, I don't like them. I don't like girl groups. I like country and western, and I like classical music.
Jane	I hate country and western, and I don't know much classical music! Do you like love films?
Paul	No, I don't. I think they are silly. But I like horror films.
Jane	Oh dear. I don't like horror films! We don't like the same things!
Paul	Well, I like Italian food. Do you?
Jane	Yes, I do. I often eat it. I love Pizza and spaghetti. I don't like fast food.
Paul	We both like Italian food and we don't like fast food. That is a start!

1 Answer the questions. | Beantworten Sie die Fragen. Exercise

a) Do you like football?
b) Do you like country and western music?
c) Do you like horror films?
d) Do you like Italian food?
e) What sport do you like?
f) What sort of music do you like?
g) What sort of films do you like best?
h) Do you like hamburgers?

Grammar

The Simple Present | Präsens

The Simple Present: Wie man auf Englisch sagt, was man gewöhnlich macht, was man beruflich macht, was man mag, usw.

Aussagesatz	Frage	Kurzantwort	Verneinung	Verneinung (Kurzform)
I work in an office.	**Do I work** in an office?	Yes, **I do**. No, **I don't**.	**I do not work** in an office.	**I don't work** in an office.
You work in a factory.	**Do you work** in a factory?	Yes, **you/I do**. No, **you/I don't**.	**You do not work** in a factory.	**You don't work** in a factory.
We work at home.	**Do we work** at home?	No, **we don't**. Yes, **we do**.	**We do not work** at home.	**We don't work** at home.
They work here.	**Do they work** here?	No, **they don't**. Yes, **they do**.	**They do not work** here.	**They don't work** here.

And you!

Ask and answer questions in English. | Stellen und beantworten Sie Fragen auf Englisch.

Finden Sie heraus, ob Ihr/e Partner/in …

Eiskrem mag.
Fisch mag.
Tennis spielt.
Technomusik mag.
in einem Büro arbeitet.
in einer Fabrik arbeitet.
Pizza mag.
zu Hause arbeitet.
oft Hamburger isst.
in Deutschland wohnt.

Example/Beispiel

Do you like ice-cream? Yes, I do. I love vanilla ice-cream.
No, I don't. I don't like ice-cream at all.

34

Jane's job

Audio Text 34 | Hörtext 34

I work for Aquapure Ltd in Leeds. I am a receptionist. I answer the telephone, and connect the callers to the right person. When visitors come, I find out who they want to visit. Then I call the person on the phone. I enter data on a computer, too, or type letters.

I like my job because I meet a lot of people. It is interesting.

I get up at 7:30 and have a shower, then I drink a cup of coffee. I don't eat breakfast. I start work at 9:00 and I finish at 5:00. I have a coffee break at 10:30 and lunch at 12:00 or 12:30. I usually eat lunch in the office canteen, or sometimes I go to an Italian restaurant.

After work, I go home to my flat and relax. I watch TV or listen to music. I like pop music. I don't like classical music.

I often meet friends in the evening, and drink a glass of wine or a cup of coffee, and talk. On Saturdays I go to the disco or to the cinema.

And you!

Answer the questions. | Beantworten Sie die Fragen.

a) When do you get up?
b) What do you do then?
c) Do you eat breakfast?
d) Do you drink tea or coffee?
e) When do you start work / school?
f) When do you finish work?
g) What do you do in the evening?
h) Do you go to the disco on Saturdays?

Grammar

Man verwendet das Simple Present, wenn man von etwas spricht, das jeden Tag oder oft passiert, vor allem bei den folgenden „Schlüsselwörtern": *always* (immer), *never* (nie), *often* (oft), *sometimes* (manchmal), *usually* (gewöhnlich), *normally* (normalerweise) und bei *every day*, *on Mondays* und so weiter sowie bei Verben wie "live" oder "work", wenn man darüber spricht, wo man wohnt oder was man beruflich macht. Wenn man seinen Alltag beschreibt, sagt man also: I **get up** … I **go** to work … I **work** …

Exercise

2 Now make the questions. | Jetzt stellen Sie Fragen.

Example/Beispiel

I like football. > Do you like football?

I live in England.
I have a big house and a fast car.
They work in London.
We often go to Switzerland in winter.
They usually go to Italy in summer.
I drink champagne every evening.

3 Now make negative sentences. | Jetzt bilden Sie verneinte Sätze.

Example/Beispiel

I like football. > I don't like football.

We love hip-hop.
They read the newspaper every morning.
We speak very good English.
I always go to bed early.
You smoke sixty cigarettes a day.
I drink a bottle of whisky every day.

Bis auf wenige Ausnahmen benötigt man im Englischen das Hilfsverb "do", um Fragen und Verneinungen zu bilden.
"Like you ice-cream?" geht nicht; die Frage lautet: "Do you like ice-cream?"
Die Ausnahmen sind: am/is/are/was/were/can/could/will/would/must.
"Do you understand?" bedeutet wörtlich übersetzt: „Tust du verstehen?" Natürlich übersetzt man das Wort "do" nicht ins Deutsche, es hört sich blöd an, oder? Aber genauso blöd hört es sich für einen Engländer an, wenn Sie fragen "Understand you?".

35

Small talk in the office

Audio Text 35 | Hörtext 35

Ann	Well, Brian, I'm afraid Mr Smith is in a meeting now, he will be back in about ten minutes.
Brian	No problem. I'm early. I'll wait.
Ann	Do you want a cup of tea or coffee?
Brian	Yes, a coffee please.
Ann	Do you take milk and sugar?
Brian	Milk please, but no sugar.
Ann	Here you are.
Brian	Thanks.
Ann	Nice day, isn't it?
Brian	Yes, lovely. I think I'll play golf this evening,
Ann	Do you often play golf?
Brian	No, I don't often have time. But I like sport. Do you do much sport?
Ann	I often play tennis in the summer, and I go for walks but I never play golf!
Brian	I sometimes go for walks, too.
Ann	Do you live in Leeds?
Brian	No, I live near Leeds, in Otley.
Ann	Oh, really? I live there too.
Brian	Do you? It is a nice village, isn't it.
Ann	Yes, we all like it.
Brian	Do you have children?
Ann	Yes, two boys. They go to Otley school. Do you have kids?
Brian	Yes, two girls. They go to Otley school too.
Ann,	Oh really. Which forms are they in?
Brian	They are both in Form 3 C. They are twins. Which forms are your sons in?
Ann	They are in Form 3 B and Form 4 C.
John	Hello, Brian. Sorry I'm late.
Brian	No problem, John. I'm chatting with your assistant. We come from the same village.

Business Tip

Small Talk ist sehr wichtig, schließlich kann es sehr unangenehm sein, sich minutenlang anzuschweigen. Heikle Themen wie Politik oder Religion sind dabei allerdings tabu.

Exercise

4 How many key words for simple present can you find in the text? | Wie viele Schlüsselwörter für Simple Present finden Sie im Text?

5 Answer the questions. | Beantworten Sie die Fragen.

How long do Ann and Mr Clark have to wait for John Smith?
Where do Ann and Mr Clark live?
Do they both have children?

Now you talk! | Jetzt reden Sie!

1 Answer

Do you like tea or coffee?
Do you take milk in coffee?
Do you take sugar in coffee?
Do you do sport?
Do you play golf?
What do you play?
Where do you live?
Do you have children?
Do they go to school?

2 Speak in English. Find out from your partner:

- ob er/sie in dieser Stadt wohnt.
- ob er/sie in einem Büro arbeitet.
- ob er/sie eine Tasse Tee möchte.
- ob er/sie um 7:00 aufsteht.
- ob er/sie Katzen mag.
- ob er/sie in Diskos geht.
- ob er/sie ein Auto hat.

Now ask each other more questions. | **Stellen Sie einander weitere Fragen.**

3 Speak in English. Find out from your partner:

- woher er/sie kommt.
- was er/sie gerne zum Frühstück isst.
- wo er/sie wohnt.
- was sein/ihr Lieblingsessen ist.
- wann er/sie nach Hause geht.
- wann er/sie mit der Arbeit anfängt.
- wann er/sie sonntags aufsteht.
- warum er/sie Englisch lernen will.
- wie viele Brüder oder Schwestern er/sie hat.
- wie viel Zucker er/sie in seinen/ihren Tee tut.

4 Now ask each other more questions.

a) Talk about your typical day: | **Beschreiben Sie Ihren Tagesablauf:**

I get up at ______, then I ______
I have breakfast at ______
I eat ______ I drink ______
I go to school/work by car/by bus/by train/on foot.
I work in an office/factory/shop. I don't work, I am a school-student.
I have lunch in a restaurant / in the canteen / in my office.
______

b) Say two things you do and two things you don't do. | **Nennen Sie zwei Dinge, die Sie häufig machen, und zwei, die Sie nicht machen.**

Example/Beispiel

I often play tennis but I don't play golf.
I usually drink tea but I don't take milk in it.

c) How often do you do it? | **Wie oft tun Sie das?**

drink tea	drink coffee	drink beer	eat cake
write letters	send e-mails	make phone calls	send SMSs
take photographs	speak English	sleep in your bed	sleep in a tent
ride a bike	ride a horse	ride an elephant	go to a disco
go to the cinema	play cards	read the paper	watch the news

never	seldom	not often	sometimes
often	usually	normally	always

d) Complete for yourself: | **Ergänzen Sie:**

I like ______ but I don't like ______
I often go to ______ but I don't often go to ______
I always read ______ but I never read ______
I want to ______ next week, but I don't want to ______

Phone!

Sie lernen:

telefonisch ein Hotelzimmer zu reservieren.

Booking a room

Audio Text 36 | Hörtext 36

36

Hotel receptionist	Good afternoon, London Bridge Hotel, how can I help you?
Ann	Hello. Do you have rooms free in the first week of July?
Hotel receptionist	One moment please: yes, you are lucky. We have two double rooms and three single rooms. The rooms are free all week, from Monday July 3rd to Sunday July 9th.
Ann	I want to book two single rooms from Monday, July 3rd to Thursday 6th, in the morning. That is, for three nights. We will be in London for three nights.
Hotel receptionist	Yes, that is OK.
Ann	Do all the rooms have bathroom and toilet in the room?
Hotel receptionist	Yes, of course. All our rooms have bathrooms. There is a mini-bar and a television in each room, too.
Ann	How much is a single room per night?
Hotel receptionist	£85, with breakfast. Continental breakfast with toast and jam and coffee is included. An English breakfast with egg and bacon is extra.
Ann	It is not cheap! But it is OK. London is expensive.
Hotel receptionist	Do you want to reserve the rooms?
Ann	Yes, please. We will arrive on the Monday morning. We don't want an English breakfast.
Hotel receptionist	Please give me your name.
Ann	The rooms are for me, my name is Ann Jones, and my colleague, John Smith. We are from the company "Aquapure Ltd".

Exercise

6 Answer the questions below. | **Beantworten Sie die folgenden Fragen.**

a) Who will stay in the rooms?
b) When do they want the rooms?
c) How many rooms are free?
d) How many rooms do they want?
e) What do all the rooms have?

7 Give the English for: | **Übersetzen Sie ins Englische:**

Haben Sie Zimmer frei?
Ich will drei Zimmer reservieren.
Haben die Zimmer Bad und WC?
Was kostet ein Einzelzimmer für eine Nacht?

Grammar

Will = werden I will go to work tomorrow.
Want to = wollen I want to go to the beach tomorrow.

Bitte verwechseln Sie diese Verben nicht, denn sonst könnte Ihr Gesprächspartner den Eindruck gewinnen, Sie möchten ihn herumkommandieren:
I will meet you tomorrow. = Ich werde Sie morgen treffen (ob Sie wollen oder nicht).
I want to meet you tomorrow. = Ich möchte Sie morgen treffen.

Exercise

Questions and answers

8 Find the right answers. | **Finden Sie die richtigen Antworten.**

Who do you want to speak to?	We want to fly to New York.
How many rooms do you want to book?	Mary Day, please.
Where do you want to fly to?	Tomorrow evening.
Do you want rooms with bathrooms?	Breakfast? I don't know.
How long do you want to stay?	Yes, of course, with bathroom and toilet.
What time do you want to have breakfast?	Two rooms, one double and one single.
Do you want breakfast?	For two nights.
When will you arrive?	At 7:30 please.

A phone conversation

9 Translate the German sentences. | **Übersetzen Sie die deutschen Sätze.**

A Mit wem wollen Sie sprechen?
B I want to speak to Mr Anderson, please.
A Tut mir leid. Er ist im Moment nicht erreichbar. Er wird heute nicht im Büro sein. Wollen Sie eine Nachricht hinterlassen?
B No, but when can I reach him? Will he be available this evening?
A Ja, aber er wird zu Hause sein. Haben Sie seine Handynummer? Wollen Sie sie haben?
B Yes, please.
A Einen Moment, bitte. Ich gebe sie Ihnen.

Write!

Sie lernen:

einen Brief zu gestalten.

Layout of a letter | Gestaltung eines Briefes

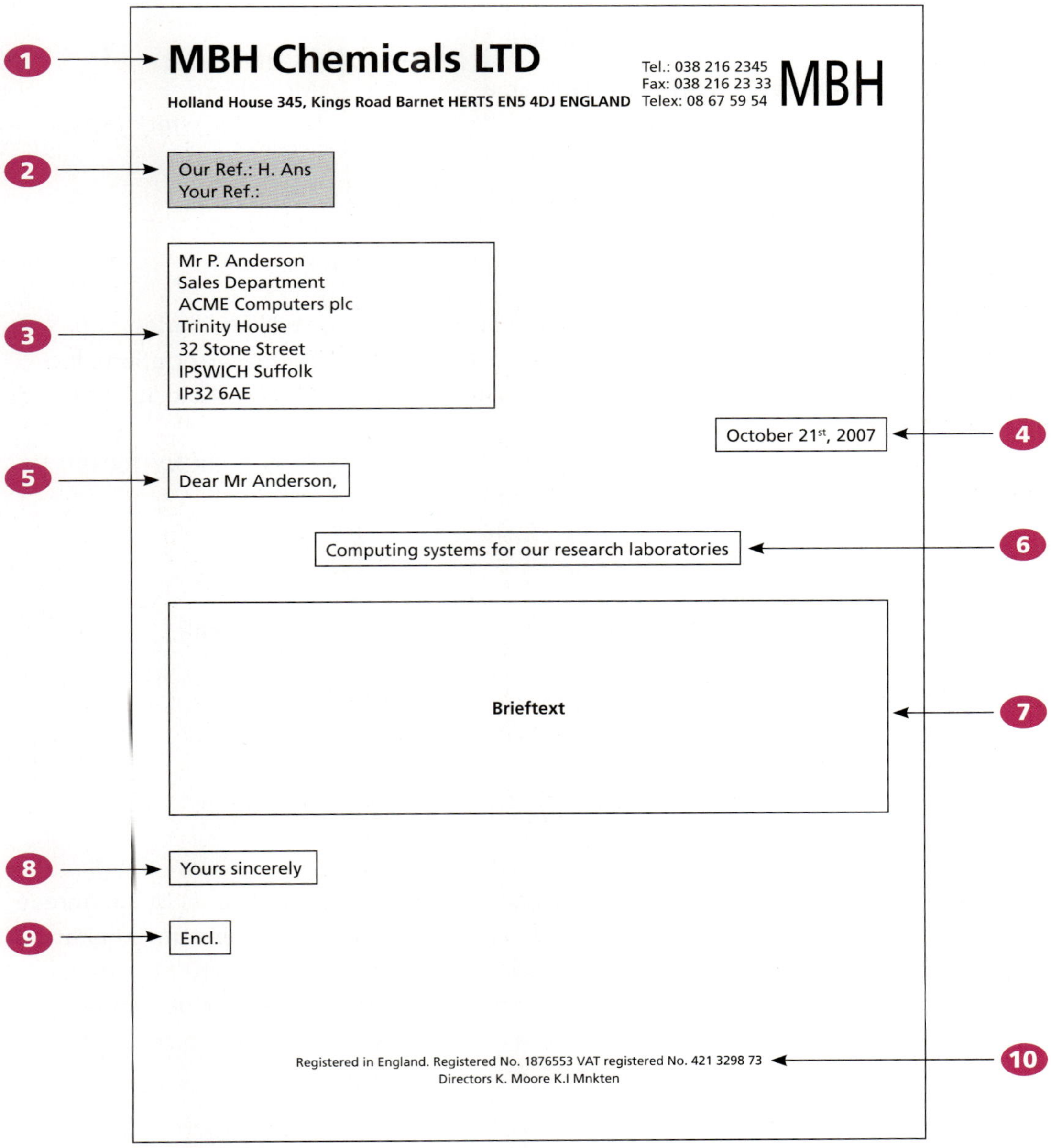

1 Letterhead | Briefkopf
Firmen verwenden in der Regel gedrucktes Briefpapier.

2 References (your ref./our ref.) | Ref./Bezugszeile
Kürzel, durch die ein Brief zugeordnet werden kann (Initialen des Verfassers und/oder der Schreibkraft usw.)

3 The address | Die Adresse
Regeln:
- Bitte halten Sie sich ganz genau an die Ihnen vorliegende Adresse.
- Jede Angabe (Name, Stadt etc.) steht in einer eigenen Zeile. Am Ende dieser Zeile bitte niemals Komma oder Punkt setzen.
- Im Englischen steht die Hausnummer vor dem Straßennamen.
- Die Namen von Straßen oder Städten bitte niemals übersetzen.
- Das Bestimmungsland so schreiben, dass es im Land des Absenders verständlich ist.
- Ort und Land in Großbuchstaben.
- Postleitzahl nicht vergessen.

Beispiel für eine Adresse in Großbritannien:

Anrede – Initiale des Vornamens – Nachname	Mr J Bloom
Hausnummer und Straße	18-22 Blackstock Mews
Ort	LONDON
Postleitzahl	N4 2B T
(von Deutschland aus: das Bestimmungsland)	ENGLAND

Beispiel für eine Adresse in den USA:

Der Vorname wird meistens vollständig angegeben.	Ms Ellen Charles
In der Adresse finden sich auch Kommas und Punkte.	D.M.A. Associations, Inc.
Manchmal ist die Angabe des betreffenden Stockwerks erforderlich.	15 West 42nd St, 25th Floor
Stadt und Postleitzahl stehen in **einer** Zeile.	NEW YORK NY 10036
Anstelle des vollständigen Namens ist die Abkürzung USA üblich.	USA

4 The date | Das Datum
Das Datum steht für gewöhnlich unter der Adresse auf der rechten Seite.

5 The greeting | Die Anrede
Briefe beginnen grundsätzlich mit "dear":

Dear Sir = Sehr geehrter Herr
Dear Mr Jones = Sehr geehrter Herr Jones
Dear Ted = Lieber Ted

"Mr" (+ Nachname) ist die Anrede für einen Mann; "Mrs" (+ Nachname) ist die Anrede für eine verheiratete Frau; "Miss" (+ Nachname) ist die Anrede für eine unverheiratete Frau. Allerdings werden letztere ("Mrs" und "Miss") zunehmend durch **"Ms"** ersetzt, da viele Frauen diese neutrale Form der Anrede vorziehen. Kennen Sie den Adressaten persönlich, ist es sowohl in Großbritannien als auch in den USA üblich, diesen mit Vornamen anzureden.

Wenn der Brief an zwei oder mehr männliche Adressaten, bzw. eine Partnerschaft (Rechtsanwaltskanzlei o. Ä.) gerichtet ist, ist "Messrs" (Plural von "Mr") als Anrede zu wählen. "Mmes" ist die Abkürzung von "Mesdames" und wird verwendet, wenn der Brief an zwei oder mehr Frauen gerichtet ist. In Briefen an Kapitalgesellschaften (Plc) ist die korrekte Anrede "Dear Sirs" (und nicht "Messrs" oder "Mmes"), wenn der Brief an keine bestimmte Person gerichtet ist, oder einfach "Dear Sir", "Dear Madam". Alternativ kann die neutrale Anrede auch "Ladies and Gentlemen" sein.

6 The subject heading | Die Betreffzeile

In englischsprachigen Briefen wird die Betreffzeile zwischen Anrede und eigentlichen Brieftext gesetzt. Die Betreffzeile besteht in geschäftlichen Briefen oft nur aus einer Rechnungs- oder Kundennummer und wird unterstrichen (underlined).

7 The body of the letter | Brieftext

Das erste Wort des eigentlichen Textes wird grundsätzlich großgeschrieben.

8 The complimentary close | Die Schlussformel

Diese richtet sich nach der Anrede.

Salutation	Close	
	British	American
Dear John	Yours sincerely Best regards	Kind regards Best regards
Dear Mr Jones	Yours sincerely	Sincerely yours Best regards
Dear Sir	Yours faithfully	Sincerely (yours)
Dear Sirs	Yours faithfully	
Ladies and Gentlemen		Yours truly

9 Enclosures | Anlagen

Fügen Sie Ihrem Schreiben Anlagen bei, sollte dies am Ende des Briefes ausdrücklich angemerkt werden. Dem deutschen Wort „Anlagen" entspricht das englische "Enclosures" („Beigefügtes"). Oft wird es abgekürzt: Enc., Encl. oder Encs. (Mz).

10 The trade name | Die Firmenbezeichnung

Die Firmenbezeichnung bwz. die Geschäftsangaben sollten an den unteren Seitenrand gesetzt werden.

Exercise

Vocabulary Practice

10 Give the opposites. | Nennen Sie das Gegenteil.

• always • seldom • interesting • early • cheap

11 Match the words which go together, sometimes, more than one answer can be right. | Setzen Sie die Wörter zusammen, die zusammengehören.

single	name
family	room
personal	job
office	computer

12 Put the verbs with the right nouns. | Ordnen Sie den Verben die passenden Substantive zu.

You can:

play	a letter
go	tennis
write	a photograph
take	golf
drink	to a disco
	for a walk
	a cup of coffee
	water

13 Make a list of English words which have to do with travel. | Machen Sie eine Liste englischer Wörter, die mit Reisen zu tun haben.

14 Give possible answers: | Welche Anwortmöglichkeiten kennen Sie?

Good afternoon	
Good bye	
Thank you very much	
How are you?	

7 Routines

Speak!

Sie lernen:

über Routinearbeiten und Arbeitsverfahren zu sprechen (Simple Present 2).

Typical days

Audio Text | Hörtext 37

37

Read and listen to the text. | **Lesen und hören Sie den Text.**

Ann I work in an office. My brother Tony works on a plane. I am an assistant in a sales office, he is an air steward. He works for an Irish airline. I start work at 8:00 or at 9:00, but he starts work at different times, sometimes at 5:00 a.m. and sometimes late in the afternoon. I work hard, but Tony works very hard, too. He gets the passenger list from the check-in desk. Then he checks the boarding cards and welcomes the passengers on the plane.

Tony talks to the passengers. He tells them what to do in an emergency. Then he sees that all passengers fasten their seat belts. When the plane is in the air, he and his colleagues bring coffee, drinks and snacks, and sell perfumes and cigarettes. Tony likes his job. He loves travelling to different countries. I don't like flying, so his job is not for me! I want a nice safe job in my office, but Tony doesn't want to sit at a desk all day. My husband Tim doesn't want an office job, either. He is a teacher.

What do we do in our free time? I go jogging or play tennis. Tony flies small planes. He has a pilot's licence, but not for passenger planes.

Exercise

1 Answer the questions below. | **Beantworten Sie die folgenden Fragen.**

a) What does Tony do?
b) Why does he like his job?
c) What does he do every day?
d) Does Ann want her brother's job?
e) Who is Tim and what is his job?
f) What does Ann do in her free time?
g) What does Tony do in his free time?
h) What do you do in your free time?

Grammar

Simple Present | Präsens

Aussagesatz	Frage	Kurzantwort	Verneinung	Verneinung (Kurzform)
I work in an office.	**Do I work** in an office?	Yes, **I do**. No, **I don't**.	**I do not work** in an office.	**I don't work** in an office.
You work in a factory.	**Do you work** in a factory?	Yes, **you/I do**. No, **you/I don't**.	**You do not work** in a factory.	**You don't work** in a factory.
He works on a plane.	**Does he work** on a plane?	Yes, **he does**. No, **he doesn't**.	**He does not work** on a plane.	**He doesn't work** on a plane.
She works in the garden.	**Does she work** in the garden?	Yes, **she does**. No, **she doesn't**.	**She does not work** in the garden.	**She doesn't work** in the garden.
It works.	**Does it work?**	Yes, **it does**. No, **it doesn't**.	**It does not work.**	**It doesn't work.**
We work at home.	**Do we work** at home?	No, **we don't**. Yes, **we do**.	**We do not work** at home.	**We don't work** at home.
They work here.	**Do they work** here?	No, **they don't**. Yes, **they do**.	**They do not work** here.	**They don't work** here.

Exercise

2 Put in the correct form of the verb. | Fügen Sie die korrekte Verbform ein.

a) I (like) ____________ flying.
b) John (work) ____________ here.
c) We (get) ____________ up at 7:00.
d) The new secretary (come) ____________ to work by car.
e) Ann and Jane (like) ____________ pop music.
f) The PC (store) ____________ the data.

→→ Bei *he, she, it:* "s" muss mit! (Diese Regel gilt nur für Simple Present.)
Bei Fragen und Verneinungen betrifft das ausschließlich das Hilfsverb "do"; z. B. "Does she like tennis? – No, she doesn't."

Exercise

3 Put in the negative. | Verneinen Sie.

a) Tony works in an office.
b) Ann likes flying.
c) The steward flies the plane.
d) The pilot sells perfume.
e) Ann and Tony live in Paris.
f) They go to school.

4 Make questions as in the example. | **Bilden Sie Fragen wie im Beispiel.**

Example/Beispiel

He plays golf > Does he play golf?

a) He eats chicken.
b) She likes flying.
c) Ann works hard.
d) The bus goes to Manchester.
e) Ann and Paul drink coffee.
f) Jane drinks tea.
g) You speak English.
h) They sell computers.

5 Make questions as in the examples. | **Stellen Sie Fragen wie in den Beispielen.**

Example/Beispiel

John lives in Leeds.	Where does John live?
He reads "The Times" every day.	What does he read every day?

a) Jane listens to pop music.
b) Paul likes classical music.
c) Ann drinks coffee at breakfast time.
d) John smokes Cuban cigars.
e) Paul comes from Germany.
f) Ann gets up at 10:00 on Sundays.
g) She has brunch in a nice pub.
h) Jane goes to the disco on Saturdays.

Now you talk! I Jetzt reden Sie!

1 Find out how often your partner does these things. | **Finden Sie heraus, wie oft Ihr Partner diese Dinge tut.**

• play football • watch football • eat Sushi • listen to Mozart • play the guitar • watch DVDs • go jogging • buy chocolate • (think of more activities!)

2 Compare with yourself. I **Vergleichen Sie mit sich selbst.**

Example/Beispiel

I often play football but he/she never plays football.

3 Describing a person I **Personenbeschreibung**

Read the description below then describe somebody you know.

My Aunt Amy is seventy, but she still works. She is a writer.
She writes books for children.
She loves children! She has twelve grandchildren. Her husband, Uncle James, is dead so she lives alone with her dogs and her cats. She says that her pets give her ideas for new books. She gets up at 7:00 every day. She works at her PC for five hours every day, then she always goes for a walk. She often visits friends in the village, and she usually meets some of them for lunch at the village pub.

4 Learning by playing.

"Who is it?" I **„Wer ist das?"**

(Schüler/-in X denkt an eine noch lebende Person, die vermutlich allen Anwesenden bekannt ist. Durch Fragen auf Englisch, die nur mit "does" gestellt werden und nur mit "yes" oder "no" beantwortet werden soll, müssen die anderen herausfinden, an wen Schüler/-in X denkt.)

Example/Beispiel

Does he/she live in the USA?
Does he/she play tennis?

Information round

Work in a groups of 3 – 6 people. I Arbeiten Sie in Gruppen von drei bis sechs Personen.
Schüler A sagt Schüler B, welche Frage er stellen soll; z.B. „Fragen Sie, wann sie aufsteht."

Schüler B stellt Schüler C die Frage auf Englisch:	*When do you get up?*
Schüler C antwortet.	*I get up at 6:00.*
Schüler D sagt der Gruppe, wann A aufsteht.	*He gets up at 6:00.*

Phone!

Sie lernen:

über Produkte Fragen zu stellen und Antworten zu geben.

Four business calls

38

Audio Text | Hörtext 38

Read and listen to all four calls. | Lesen und hören Sie alle vier Anrufe.

Call 1

Caller 1	I want information about the new TP 3 printer. How much does it cost?
Ann	It costs £67.50
Caller 1	Sixty-seven pounds and fifty pence?
Ann	That is right.
Caller 1	Does it have a full guarantee?
Ann	Yes, of course, it has a guarantee for two years. It is a first-class machine!
Caller 1	How much ink does it use?
Ann	It uses less ink than the TP2 printer. Visit our web-site for exact figures.
Caller 1	Do you give a discount for big orders? My company wants fifteen printers.
Ann	Yes, we can give you 3% on an order for 15 printers.
Caller 1	Thanks. I want to think about it.
Ann	Can I have your name please?
Caller 1	Harry Potts.

Call 2

Caller 2	Hello, hello, is that the hot-line?
Brian	Yes, what is the problem?
Caller 2	My PC doesn't work.
Brian	What is your name? What is your customer number?
Caller 2	Mary Smith. CC 7432.
Brian	OK. Now, tell me, what does the PC do?
Caller 2	Nothing! It doesn't start!

Call 3

Caller 3	I want information about the computer course in April. When does it start?
Ann	It starts on April 10th at 9:00.
Caller	When does it finish?
Ann	It finishes at 16:30 on April 12th.
Caller 3	Is it for beginners?
Ann	Yes, it is.
Caller 3	How much does it cost?
Ann	It costs £90 for the three days.
Caller 3	Can I register for the course now?
Ann	Yes, of course. Please tell me your name.
Caller 3	Manfred Bayer.

Call 4

Caller 4	Hello, I'm phoning about the second-hand bike for sale.
Jane	Hello, my name is Jane. I want to sell the bike. What do you want to know?
Caller 4	How old is the bike?
Jane	It is only two years old.
Caller 4	I see. How many gears does it have?
Jane	It has 17 gears.
Caller 4	Do the brakes work?
Jane	Yes, they do. The brakes work very well.
Caller 4	Can I come and look at it?
Jane	Yes, you can. Do you want to come this evening?
Caller 4	Yes, my name is Rose Hines.
Jane	OK, my address is 17, Rushmere Avenue. Can you come at about 7:00?
Caller 4	Yes, see you then.

Exercise

6 Answer the questions. | Beantworten Sie die Fragen.

a) Who wants information about a printer? (Give the name.)
b) How much does the TP3 printer cost?
c) Who has problems with her computer?
d) What does her computer do?
e) Who asks about the computer course?
f) Who is the course for?
g) How long is it?
h) Who wants to buy a bike?
i) Where is the bike?

7 Find the English for: | Finden Sie die englischen Entsprechungen für:

Ich rufe wegen des Fahrrads an.
Ich möchte mich über den neuen Drucker erkundigen.
Besuchen Sie unsere Website, um genaue Zahlen zu erfahren.
Geben Sie einen Mengenrabatt?

Asking for information on the phone

Now you phone! | Jetzt telefonieren Sie!

You	Ich rufe wegen des Kurses „Englisch für Geschäftsleute" an.
	➤ Yes, what do you want to know?
You	Wann fängt der Kurs an?
	➤ On Monday, September 10th
You	Bis wann läuft er?
	➤ Until Monday, November 17th.
You	Wie viel kostet er?
	➤ £200 for fifteen double-hours.
You	Danke. Ich möchte es mir noch überlegen. Auf Wiederhören.

And you!

Choose an article from the list below. | **Wählen Sie einen Artikel aus der unten stehenden Liste.**

Partner A wants to sell it his/her article.
Partner B wants to buy it.
Partner B rings up and asks about it.

• bike • inline-skates • laptop • smart car • Hi-fi system • video-player • camera • mobile phone

Write!

Sie lernen:

Anfragen zu schreiben und/oder zu beantworten.

Exercise

8 Read the sentences and translate them into German. | **Lesen Sie die Sätze und übersetzen Sie sie ins Deutsche.**

Subject: Enquiry[1] about ...

a) I am writing to ask about ...
b) We are looking for ...
c) Please find enclosed our specifications.
d) Please send me your catalogue and price list.
e) We/I look forward to hearing from you.

Subject: Your enquiry about ...

f) Thank you for your letter of June 20th.
g) In reply to your letter of 30 July ...
h) Please find enclosed our catalogue and price list.
i) Please find enclosed our offer.
j) If you have any questions please contact us/me.
k) I look forward to your order.

9 Now you write! | Jetzt schreiben Sie!

Schreiben Sie einen Brief an Herrn Brian Day, Office Equipment Plc, Church Street, Ipswich IPS 32 P. Sie wollen sich nach Bürostühlen erkundigen. Schreiben Sie in Ihrem eigenen Namen und mit dem heutigen Datum. Sie möchten einen Katalog und die Preisliste haben. Formulieren Sie auch seine Antwort, mit Katalog und Preisliste als Anlagen.

[1] enquiry = Anfrage

Vocabulary Practice

Exercise

1. The business letter starts "Dear Ann"; how should it close?
   A love and kisses
   B yours faithfully
   C best regards
2. Ellen Crow is a top manager. You do not know her personally. She was married but is divorced. You write her a letter. How do you address her?
   A Ms Crow
   B Miss Ellen
   C Mrs Manager Crow
3. You want to sell your bike on eBay. It isn't new, so how do you describe it?
   A second-hand
   B first-hand
   C third-class
4. A letter asking for information about a product can be called
   A an asker
   B an invitation
   C an enquiry
5. You send your catalogue with a letter; what do you write in the letter?
   A Please find somewhere my catalogue.
   B Please look for the attachment.
   C Please find enclosed our catalogue.

8 Yesterday

Speak!

Sie lernen:

über die Vergangenheit zu sprechen.

39 Monday morning

Audio Text 39 | Hörtext 39

It is Monday morning. John comes into the office. He is very brown!

Ann	Hello, John: Wow, you are brown! Where were you at the weekend? Were you in Italy?
John	No, I was in England. I was at the seaside with Emily and the children. We were on the beach all day yesterday and the day before yesterday.
Ann	I can see the weather was good!
John	Yes, the sun was hot. But the wind was cool. It was great! Where were you last weekend, Ann?
Ann	I was here in Leeds. It wasn't sunny, but I was with friends. It was a nice weekend.
John	And you, Paul. How was your weekend?
Paul	It was OK. But I was at a disco on Saturday, and I was in bed until yesterday afternoon!

Exercise

1 Answer the questions. | Beantworten Sie die Fragen.

Where is John now?
Where was he at the weekend?
Was Paul at the seaside?
Where was he on Saturday evening?
Was Ann at a disco?

And you!

Find out about your partner: Where was he/she last weekend? | **Finden Sie über ihre/n Partner/in heraus, wo er/sie am Wochenende war.**

a) Where were you last Saturday?
b) When were you last in a disco?
c) Where were you on Sunday?
d) Where was your best friend last weekend?

Ask each other more questions with "was" and "were". | **Stellen Sie einander weitere Fragen mit "was" and "were".**

Grammar

The past tense of "be" | Präteritum

I/he/she/it	**was**	→ I was at home yesterday, he was at home, too.
you/we/they	**were**	→ We were at home yesterday.

I am at home today, I was at home yesterday. He is at home today, he was at home yesterday.
I wasn't at the disco. Was she at the disco? No, she wasn't there.

Exercise

2 am/is/are/was or were? | am/is/are/was oder were?

a) I ______ on holiday in Majorca last month, but now I ______ at home again.
b) It ______ sunny this morning, but yesterday it ______ rainy.
c) My parents ______ at home last week, but now they ______ on holiday.
d) We ______ in London in 1999 and we ______ in Paris in 2000.
e) ______ you busy now? Yes, I ______

3 Read the following text. Underline the past tense forms. | **Lesen Sie den folgenden Text. Unterstreichen Sie das Präteritum.**

John Smith went to the seaside last weekend. He sat on the sand with his wife and he played with his children. They made sandcastles, and they swam in the sea. He had a nice time.
Ann had a nice time too. She stayed in Leeds. She met some friends. They talked and then they went to an Italian restaurant. Then they watched a film on TV.
Paul went to a disco on Saturday, with Jane. They danced a lot. He came home late and slept late on Sunday. He got up at 11:30.

Exercise

4 Give the infinitive form. | Nennen Sie die Grundform.

Unregelmäßige Verben		Regelmäßige Verben	
Infinitive	**Past**	**Infinitive**	**Past**
go	went		played
	sat		stayed
	made		talked
	swam		watched
	had		danced
	met		
	came		
	slept		
	got		

5 Put the verbs in brackets into the past. | Setzen Sie die Verben in Klammern in die Vergangenheitsform.

a) Paul (go) ______ to the disco on Saturday last week, and (come) ______ home very late.
b) He (get up) ______ at half past eleven last Sunday.
c) He (shave) ______ and (have) ______ a shower.
d) Then he (get) ______ dressed and (have) ______ a cup of coffee.
e) He (go) ______ jogging in the park.
f I (get) ______ your e-mail yesterday. Here is the information you asked for.

Regelmäßige Verben = Wortstamm + ed

base form	simple past	
work	worked	Stamm + ed
stop	sto**pp**ed	Nach kurzem Vokal wird der Mitlaut verdoppelt.
carry	carr**ie**d	Nach Mitlaut, wird **y** zu **ie**, **aber nicht nach a/e/i/o/u**.

Jane's jobs

Exercise

Her new job | **Her old job**

6 Put in the missing verbs in the past tense. | **Ergänzen Sie die fehlenden Verben in past tense.**

Example/Beispiel

Her new job	Her old job
Now Jane works for Aquapure Ltd.	Last year she worked for a small firm.
Jane's new boss is John Smith.	Her old boss was Mrs Miller.

Fill in the gaps (the following are regular verbs).

a) Jane lives in a flat in Leeds now.	She lived with her mother in Manchester.
b) She earns more money now.	She _______________ less in her old job.
c) She starts work at 9:00.	She _______________ work at 8:30.
d) She finishes work at 5:30.	She _______________ work at 5:00.

Fill in the gaps (the following are irregular verbs).

a) She sees a lot of people.	She only ___________ one or two colleagues.
b) She sits at the reception desk.	She ___________ in a small office.
c) She goes to work by bus.	She ___________ to work by train.
d) She gets up at 7:00.	She ___________ up at 6:00.

7 Complete: | **Ergänzen Sie:**

I usually go to an Italian restaurant, but last Saturday I ___________ to a Greek restaurant.
My boss usually comes at 9:00 but yesterday he ___________ at 10:00.
I often watch horror films but last night I ___________ a love film.
We usually have toast for breakfast, but yesterday we ___________ corn flakes.
She usually sees a lot of people, and today she ___________ a lot of people, too.
He usually sleeps in a bed, but last weekend he ___________ on the sofa.

Grammar

Im Simple Present bildet man Fragen und Verneinungen mit **do/does**;
im Simple Past mit **did** (Vgl. Seite 68).

Aussagesatz	Frage (did + Grundform)	Verneinung
I went	Did I go?	I didn't go.
you came	Did you come?	You didn't come.
he worked	Did he work?	He didn't work.
she phoned	Did she phone?	She didn't phone.
it stopped	Did it stop?	It didn't stop.
we wrote	Did we write?	We didn't write.
they answered	Did they answer?	They didn't answer.

Wie man das Simple Past bildet, haben Sie schon gelernt (vgl. Seite 90). Aber um Frage und Verneinung zu bilden, verwendet man das Hilfsverb "did" (= Simple Past von "do") plus Grundform; z. B. "He went. Did he go? He didn't go."

Exercise

8 Make the questions. | Stellen Sie Fragen.

a)	He went to Berlin.	Did he go to Berlin?
b)	He visited a customer.	
c)	She phoned.	
d)	The bus stopped.	
e)	They wrote a letter.	
f)	He answered.	
g)	I came.	

9 Fill in the gaps. | Füllen Sie die Lücken aus.

He didn't go to Berlin, he went to Paris.
She didn't write an e-mail, she ________ a letter.
I didn't meet Ann, I ________ Jane.
He didn't come at 9:00, he ________ at 10:00.
You didn't phone me, you ________ Ann.

10 Put the right answers with the questions. | Ordnen Sie den Fragen die richtigen Antworten zu.

When was your last holiday?	I went there with my family.
Where did you go?	My last holiday was last July.
Who did you go with?	I went to Sylt.
Where did you stay?	I liked swimming in the sea.
What was the flat like?	We stayed in a holiday flat.
What did you like doing there?	When it rained it was boring. There was nothing to do.
Did you do anything new?	I learned how to surf. That was fun.
What didn't you like?	It was a good holiday, the weather was good most of the time.
Was the holiday good or bad?	The flat was nice but small.

And you!

Ask your partner all the questions.
Answer the questions.
Talk about your holiday.

Stellen Sie Ihrem Partner alle oben genannten Fragen.

Now you talk! | Jetzt reden Sie!

1 Complete. | Ergänzen Sie.

Yesterday was ______ I ______ up at ______, then I ______
and ______ I ______ ______ for breakfast.
After breakfast, I ______
In the morning, I ______
At lunchtime, I ______
In the afternoon, I ______
I finished ______ at ______ and then I ______
In the evening I ______ and ______
I went to bed at ______

2 Ask and answer. | **Stellen Sie die folgenden Fragen und beantworten Sie sie.**

a)	Did you eat spaghetti yesterday?	
b)	Did you go to the cinema last week?	
c)	Did you go to Majorca last summer?	
d)	Did you drink coffee at breakfast time?	
e)	Did you learn English at school?	

3 Say two things you did last week, and two things you didn't do. | **Nennen Sie zwei Dinge, die Sie letzte Woche getan und zwei, die Sie nicht getan haben.**

Example/Beispiel
I went to my aerobics class last week, but I didn't go swimming.
My friend saw a film last Tuesday, but I didn't see it.

PHONE!

Sie lernen:

einige typische Anrufe im Büro.

40

Did you get my e-mail?

Audio Text 40 | Hörtext 40

Read and listen to the three dialogues. | **Lesen und hören Sie die drei Dialoge.**

Dialogue 1

Ann Good morning, this is Ann Jones speaking. Can I speak to Joan Miller?
Joan Hi Ann.
Ann Hello Joan. I'm afraid I'm in a hurry. Did you get my e-mail on Monday?
Joan Yes, I got it. You said you needed information. I will send the file this afternoon.
Ann OK, thanks Joan. I need it for the meeting.

Dialogue 2

Jim Hello, Jim Jay speaking.
Joan Hello, this is Joan.
Jim Hi, Joan, how are you?
Joan Fine, but where is the file for Aquapure Ltd? I asked you for it yesterday.
Jim It sent it to you yesterday, by e-mail.
Joan Oh. Yes, here is the e-mail. Thanks Jim.

Dialogue 3

John Hi, Ann. Did you phone Mrs Miller?
Ann Yes, I phoned her this morning.
John Did she receive the e-mail?
Ann Yes, she got it.
John Good, did she send the file?
Ann Yes, she sent it. It came an hour ago.
John Please give me a copy.
Ann I printed a copy and put it on your desk half an hour ago.

Exercise

11 Underline the verbs in the past tense. | **Unterstreichen Sie die Verben in Vergangenheitsform.**

12 Find the English for: | **Finden Sie die englischen Entsprechungen für:**

Haben Sie meine E-Mail bekommen?
Ich habe es Ihnen gestern per E-Mail geschickt.
Ich habe Sie gestern darum gebeten.
Ich habe Sie gestern angerufen.

Write!

Sie lernen:

über die Vergangenheit zu berichten.

Exercise

13 Write a report in English: | Schreiben Sie einen Bericht auf Englisch:

a) about your holiday last year,

b) about what you did yesterday.

Date: ____________

Name: ____________

Activities: at ____________ a.m., I ____________ then I ____________

First I ____________ then I ____________

____

At ____________, I ____________

Finally, at ____________ I ____________

14 Put the verbs in the Simple Past. | Bilden Sie das "Simple Past" der Verben.

Report of a meeting of the Business English Study Group.

The meeting (take) ____________ place on Monday, May 29th, 2006 in room 76.
It (start) ____________ at 19:00 and (finish) ____________ at 21:00.

Topic 1: Information about a trip to England
Mrs Green (tell) ____________ the students about the group trip to England in July.
She (give) ____________ each student the address of a guest family.

Topic 2: Payment for the trip
Mrs Green (ask) ____________ all students to pay the money for the trip before June 5th.

Topic 3: Luggage for England
Mrs Green (say) ____________ that the weight limit for cases on the plane is 15 kilos.

Vocabulary Practice

Von jetzt an werden Sie Ihre Englischkenntnisse auch am Arbeitsplatz verwenden können. Natürlich ist Ihr Wortschatz noch klein, es wird viele Wörter geben, die Sie nicht verstehen. Dafür gibt es Werkzeuge und zwar Wörterbücher. Nur, wie jedes Werkzeug, muss man erstens das für seine Zwecke geeignetste kaufen und zweitens muss man wissen, wie man es richtig benutzt.

Welches Wörterbuch?
Ein elektronisches Wörterbuch in Form von Software für den PC ist natürlich sehr nützlich, wenn man viel am Computer arbeitet, da man Übersetzungen direkt in Dokumente übertragen kann. Aber Sie brauchen auch eins für unterwegs. Es gibt spezielle Sprachcomputer, in die man das gesuchte Wort eintippt und die Übersetzung auf dem Bildschirm erscheint. Die sind natürlich auch gut, doch ein Wörterbuch im Buchformat ist wesentlich preiswerter.
Sie benötigen für den eigenen Gebrauch keinen dicken Wälzer und auch kein teures Fachwörterbuch. Sie brauchen ein kleines, handliches Wörterbuch im Taschenformat. Dort werden Sie sich schneller und besser zurechtfinden. Es gibt viele solche Wörterbücher; unser Beispiel ist aus dem Langenscheidt Schulwörterbuch Englisch. Ihr Wörterbuch sollte Ihnen ähnliche Informationen geben.

Beispiel: Englisch/Deutsch
train^{1} [treIn] s Zug, go by ~ mit dem Zug fahren
train^{2} [treIn] 1 v/t trainieren, *Mitarbeiter* ausbilden, *Hund* abrichten
2 v/i *von Mannschaft, Sportler* trainieren

Eine hochgestellte Zahl	besagt, dass es zwei unterschiedliche Bedeutungen für dieses Wort gibt.
[treIn]	In den eckigen Klammern steht das Wort in Lautschrift.
s = Substantiv:	das heißt, es handelt sich um ein Nomen oder Hauptwort.
go by ~	In einer Redewendung, die ebenfalls übersetzt wird, wird das Wort, um das es geht durch ~ ersetzt; also go by train = mit dem Zug fahren.
train^{2} 1 und 2:	Diese Zahlen geben an, dass das Wort zwei miteinander verwandte Bedeutungen hat, einmal als v/t = transitives Verb (Verb mit Objekt) und einmal als v/i = intransitives Verb (Verb ohne Objekt).

Beispiel: Deutsch/Englisch
befreien v/t free; *Volk, Land* liberate
retten rescue; *von Pflichten* exempt; *vom Unterricht* excuse

An diesem Beispiel sehen wir, dass es für ein Wort mehrere Übersetzungen geben kann. Lesen Sie sich den Abschnitt im Wörterbuch gut durch, das kann dabei helfen, die richtige Übersetzung zu finden.
In einem großen Wörterbuch wäre der Abschnitt zu lang und zu kompliziert, um Ihnen zu nützen.

Vokabelverzeichnis – Chronologisch

Unit 1

speak (v)	sprechen
phone (v)	telefonieren
write (v)	schreiben
office	Büro
in the office	im Büro
contact	Kontakt
Pleased to meet you.	Erfreut, Sie kennenzulernen.
listen (to) (v)	zuhören
read (v)	lesen
the	der/die/das
text	Text
here	hier
is	ist
head office	Hauptbüro
of	von
Ltd	Eine der Rechtsformen für britische Firmen mit begrenzter Haftung
a/an	ein
British	britisch
firm	Firma
employee	Angestellte/r
water filter	Wasserfilter
new	neu
trainee	Auszubildende/r, Praktikant/in
from	von, aus
Germany	Deutschland
my	mein/e
name	Name
what	was
your	dein/e, euer, eure, Ihr/e
I	ich
I'm (I am)	ich bin
business	Geschäft
tip	Tipp
where	wo
are	sind
pardon?	Wie bitte?
German	deutsch
that	dass

right	richtig
Germany	Deutschland
Leeds	eine Stadt in Nordengland
village	Dorf
near	in der Nähe von
assistant	Assistent/in
sales department	Verkaufsabteilung
too	auch
partner	Partner/Partnerin
Introduce yourself.	Stellen Sie sich vor.
ask (v)	fragen
say (v)	sagen
English	englisch
he	er
she	sie
it	es
big	groß
city	Stadt
sale	Verkauf
work	Arbeit
they	sie (Mehrzahl)
now	jetzt
North	Norden
as … as	so … wie
sun	Sonne
hot	heiß
we	wir
boss	Chef/in
happy	glücklich
late	spät
You are late.	Du kommst zu spät.
small	klein
girl	Mädchen
work (v)	arbeiten
answer (v)	antworten/beantworten
similar	ähnlich
question	Frage
meet (v)	kennenlernen
How are you?	Wie geht es Ihnen? Wie geht es dir/euch?
how	wie

this	dies
our	unser
sales director	Verkaufsdirektor/in
How do you do?	Erfreut, Sie kennenzulernen.
Please call me John.	Bitte nennen Sie mich John.
thanks	Danke
I'm fine.	Mir geht es gut.
wrong	falsch
correct	korrigieren
if	falls
family name/last name/ surname	Familienname/ Nachname
office worker	Büroarbeiter/in
translator	Übersetzer/in
interpreter	Dolmetscher/in
accountant	Buchhalter/in
head of department	Abteilungsleiter/in
programmer	Programmierer/in
technician	Techniker/in
salesman	Verkäufer
saleswoman	Verkäuferin
teacher	Lehrer/in
receptionist	Empfangsdame/ Empfangssekretärin
director	Direktor/in
bank clerk	Bankangestellte/r
French	französisch
American	amerikanisch
Italian	italienisch
book	Buch
job	Arbeit/Aufgabe
husband	Ehemann
father	Vater
wife	Ehefrau
mother	Mutter
friend	Freund/in
doctor	Arzt/Ärztin
driver	Fahrer/in
professor	Professor/in
waiter	Kellner
waitress	Kellnerin
actor	Schauspieler

actress	Schauspielerin
Japanese	japanisch
queen	Königin
secretary	Sekretär/in
at my desk	an meinem Schreibtisch
her	ihr/e
his	sein/e
their	ihr/e
our	unser/e
who	wer
desk	Schreibtisch
nice	schön/nett
better	besser
complete (v)	ergänzen
sentence	Satz
hair	Haare
brown	braun
blue	blau
eye	Auge
plural	Mehrzahl
boy	Junge
girl	Mädchen
day	Tag
watch	Armbanduhr
bus	Bus
man/men	Mann/Männer
woman/women	Frau/Frauen
child/children	Kind/Kinder
mouse/mice	Maus/Mäuse
on	auf
at home	zu Hause
at school	in der Schule
talk (v)	reden
Now you talk!	Jetzt reden Sie!
hobby	Hobby
favourite	Lieblings-
favourite singer	Lieblingssänger/in
singer	Sänger/in
address	Adresse
learn (v)	lernen
play (v)	spielen
Learning by playing	Lernen durch Spielen
sportsman	Sportler

sportswoman	Sportlerin
racing driver	Rennfahrer/in
football	Fußball
player	Spieler/in
address	Adresse
be on the phone	gerade telefonieren
Ann speaking	Ann am Apparat
How can I help you?	Wie kann ich Ihnen helfen?
can (v)	können
please	bitte
one moment	einen Moment
I'll connect you	ich verbinde
sorry	es tut mir leid
available	erreichbar
meeting	Besprechung
I'll phone	ich werde anrufen
this afternoon	heute Nachmittag
Have a nice day!	Schönen Tag noch!
Goodbye/Bye	Auf Wiedersehen/ Auf Wiederhören
answer the phone	ein Gespräch annehmen
Good afternoon	Guten Tag
Put me through.	Stellen Sie mich durch.
The line is busy.	Die Leitung ist besetzt.
Do you want to hold on?	Wollen Sie warten?
try later (v)	(es) später versuchen
later	später
I want to …	Ich möchte … / Ich will …
I can't	Ich kann nicht
understand (v)	verstehen
repeat (v)	wiederholen
very	sehr
good	gut
Please hold the line.	Bitte warten Sie.
There is no answer.	Es geht niemand ans Telefon.
I'll send an e-mail	Ich werde eine E-Mail schicken.
I will (I'll)	ich werde
I want to	Ich will/möchte
slowly	langsam

call	Anruf
translate (v)	übersetzen
(phone) call	Anruf
another call	noch ein Anruf
call (v)	anrufen
rule	Regel
June	Juni
subject	Betreff
project	Projekt
order number	Bestellnummer
find (v)	finden
information	Information
attached file	Anhang
member	Mitglied
group	Gruppe
Best regards	Mit freundlichen Grüßen
send (v)	schicken
get (v)	bekommen
sender	Absender
receive (v)	bekommen
recipient	Empfänger
problem	Problem
with	mit
there is/there are	es gibt
a list	eine Liste
as soon as possible	so schnell wie möglich
Can we meet?	Können wir uns treffen?
next	nächste
week	Woche
give (v)	geben
Monday	Montag
morning	Morgen/Vormittag
arrange (v) a meeting	ein Treffen vereinbaren
for Friday	für Freitag
possible	möglich
if possible	wenn möglich
date	Datum
time	Uhrzeit
asap = as soon as possible	so bald wie möglich
Tuesday	Dienstag

Unit 2

here	hier
on holiday	in Urlaub
holiday	Urlaub/Ferien
at the seaside	am Meer
busy	beschäftigt
today	heute
hard	schwer
prepare (v)	vorbereiten
do (v)	tun/machen
sit (v)	sitzen
on the beach	am Strand
beside	neben
sea	Meer
sunbathe (v)	sich sonnen
magazine	Illustrierte
make (v)	machen
sand-castle	Sandburg
I wish you were here!	Ich wünschte, du wärst hier!
come (v)	kommen
evening	Abend
I'm looking forward to it.	Ich freue mich darauf.
shine (v)	scheinen
water	Wasser
warm	warm
sky	Himmel
nice	schön/nett
swim (v)	schwimmen
sail (v)	segeln
have fun (v)	Spaß haben
Give ... my love.	Viele Grüße an ...
weekend	Wochenende
See you soon.	Bis bald.
Give my regards to …	Grüß(en Sie) … von mir.
customer	Kunde/Kundin
sleep (v)	schlafen
run (v)	laufen
stop (v)	anhalten
rain (v)	regnen
drink (v)	trinken
picture	Bild
for example	zum Beispiel
eat (v)	essen
letter	Brief
photo	Foto
pretty	hübsch
like	so wie
photograph	Foto
park	Park
walk (v)	laufen/spazieren
dog	Hund
black	schwarz
white	weiß
brother	Bruder
house	Haus
son	Sohn
red	rot
there is/there are	es gibt
What is … like?	Wie ist …?
town	Stadt
but	aber
a lot of	eine Menge/viele
old	alt
market place	Marktplatz
grey	grau
stone	Stein
church	Kirche
little	klein
river	Fluss
bridge	Brücke
shop	Geschäft
supermarket	Supermarkt
restaurant	Restaurant
pub	Kneipe
café	Café
You must come.	Du musst kommen.
Sunday	Sonntag
have (v)	haben
lunch	Mittagessen
see (v)	sehen
kind	nett
railway station	Bahnhof
timetable	Fahrplan
bus station	Busbahnhof
number	Nummer

bus-stop	Bushaltestelle
student	Student/in
class	Klasse
classroom	Klassenzimmer
chair	Stuhl
table	Tisch
clock	Uhr
wall	Wand
university	Universität
shopping centre	Einkaufszentrum
theatre	Theater
youth club	Jugendzentrum
sports ground	Sportplatz
stadium	Stadion
concert hall	Konzerthalle
home town	Heimatort
bag	Tasche
watch TV (v)	fernsehen
mobile phone	Handy
ring (v)	klingeln
interesting	interessant
stay (v)	bleiben
long	lange
coffee-bar	Café
city centre	Stadtzentrum
on the way to	auf dem Weg nach
car	Auto
out of order	außer Betrieb
stop (v)	anhalten
motorway	Autobahn
mechanic	Mechaniker/in
repair (v)	reparieren
near	in der Nähe von
flat	Wohnung
See you.	Wir sehen uns.
in a few minutes	in einigen Minuten
telephone message	Telefonnachricht
message	Nachricht, Mitteilung
taken by	notiert von
free	frei
relax (v)	sich entspannen
think (v)	denken
dinner	Abendessen

report	Bericht
a lot to do	eine Menge zu tun
See you later!	Bis später!
about	über/wegen
invoice	Rechnung
incorrect	falsch/fehlerhaft
correct	korrekt/richtig
price	Preis
apologise (v)	sich entschuldigen
really	wirklich
mistake	Fehler
letter-post	Briefpost
by letter-post	mit der Post
corrected	korrigiert
bank	Bank
transfer (v)	überweisen
company	Gesellschaft
account	Konto
pay (v)	bezahlen
department store	Warenhaus
window	Fenster
cousin	Vetter/Kusine
grandmother	Großmutter
lamp	Lampe
yellow	gelb
flag	Fahne

Unit 3

lunch break	Mittagspause
time	Zeit
canteen	Kantine
What is the time?	Wie spät ist es?
open	offen
buy (v)	kaufen
cup	Tasse
cup of coffee	Tasse Kaffee
cheese roll	Käsebrötchen
hungry	hungrig
He is hungry.	Er hat Hunger.
thirsty	durstig
He is thirsty.	Er hat Durst.
ham	Schinken

pound	Pfund (britische Währung)
note	Geldschein
change	Kleingeld
milk	Milch
sugar	Zucker
expensive	teuer
menu	Speisekarte
Look!	Schauen Sie! Guck mal!
cheap	billig
from … to	von … bis
You are welcome!	Bitte/Gern geschehen!
dinner	Abendessen
film	Film
many people	viele Leute
watch (v)	zuschauen
New Year's Eve	Silvester
starter	Vorspeise
mean (v)	bedeuten
high noon	12 Uhr mittags
vote (v)	wählen
soup	Suppe
tomato	Tomate
oxtail	Ochsenschwanz
main dish	Hauptgericht
sausage	Wurst
chicken	Huhn
fried	gebraten
fish	Fisch
special	hier: Tagesmenü
roast lamb	Lammbraten
peas	Erbsen
roast potato	Röstkartoffel
mint	Minze
sauce	Soße
chips	Pommes
salad	Salat
dessert	Nachtisch/Nachspeise
ice cream	Eis
apple pie	Apfeltasche
drinks	Getränke
mineral water	Mineralwasser
apple juice	Apfelsaft
tea	Tee
week	Woche
key	Taste (u. a. am Computer)
money	Geld
pocket	Tasche
bread	Brot
stress	Stress
too many	zu viele
potato	Kartoffel
bottle	Flasche
pot	Kanne
crisps	Chips
biscuits	Kekse
piece	Scheibe
cake	Kuchen
railway company	Bahngesellschaft
ticket	Fahrkarte
single (ticket)	Einzelfahrschein
return (ticket)	Hin- und Rückfahrkarte
what?	was?
way	Weg
back	zurück
day	Tag
weekend	Wochenende
journey	Reise
form	Formular
fill in (v)	ausfüllen
copy (v)	kopieren
capital letters	Großbuchstaben
ink	Tinte
forename/first name	Vorname
date of birth	Geburtsdatum
place of birth	Geburtsort
nationality	Nationalität
occupation	Beruf
marital status	Familienstand
married	verheiratet
single	ledig
divorced	geschieden
postal code	Postleitzahl
signature	Unterschrift
breakfast	Frühstück

Unit 4

next	nächste
important	wichtig
won't (will not)	werden nicht/wird nicht
business trip	Geschäftsreise
chain	Kette
Wednesday	Mittwoch
Thursday	Donnerstag
managing director	Geschäftsführer
discuss (v)	besprechen
design department	Designabteilung
guy (slang)	Typ/Kollege
finance department	Finanzabteilung
sure	sicher
I'll ask Ann to send it.	Ich werde Ann bitten, es zu schicken.
minutes	Protokoll
tomorrow	morgen
be (v)	sein
before	vor
Saturday	Samstag
Sunday	Sonntag
some	einige
thing	Ding
fluently	fließend
piano	Klavier
play the piano (v)	Klavier spielen
winter	Winter
snow (v)	schneien
win (v)	gewinnen
world cup	Weltmeisterschaft
year	Jahr
lottery	Lotto
well	gut
He can play well.	Er kann gut spielen.
soccer/football	Fußball
rugby	Rugby
team	Mannschaft
happy	glücklich
of course	natürlich
match	Spiel
goalkeeper	Torhüter
birthday	Geburtstag

arrive (v)	ankommen
Sunday	Sonntag
That's a pity!	Schade!
like (v)	mögen
Peter likes me.	Peter mag mich.
wait (v)	warten
Wait for me!	Warten Sie auf mich!
quarter	Viertel
Give it to me!	Geben Sie es mir!
pretty	hübsch
at lunch	zu Tisch
past	nach
to	vor
half	halb
hurry (v)	sich beeilen
I must hurry.	Ich muss mich beeilen.
meet (v)	treffen
Can we meet ?	Können wir uns treffen?
reception	Rezeption/Empfang
alone	allein
must (v)	müssen
date	Rendezvous
Cheerio!	Tschüss!
Let's go!	Gehen wir!
cinema	Kino
type (v)	tippen
only	nur
a little bit	ein bisschen
dance (v)	tanzen
ride (v)	reiten
horse	Pferd
ski (v)	Skifahren
cook (v)	kochen
sing (v)	singen
sunny	sonnig
get home (v)	zu Hause ankommen
leave home (v)	das Haus verlassen
end	Ende
lesson	Klassenstunde
first	erst
every day	jeden Tag
caller	Anrufer
dialling code	Vorwahl

call back (v)	zurückrufen
He will call you back.	Er ruft Sie zurück.
after	nach
mobile (phone) number	Handynummer
try (v)	versuchen
extension number	Durchwahl
dial (v)	wählen (Telefon)
reach (v)	erreichen
When can I reach him?	Wann kann ich ihn erreichen?
check (v)	überprüfen
invitation	Einladung
room	Raum
confirm (v)	bestätigen
agenda	Tagesordnung
attached file/ attachment	Anhang (bei Briefen und E-Mails)
a little	ein bisschen
airport	Flughafen
flight	Flug
flight number	Flugnummer
collect (v)	abholen
I look forward to meeting you again.	Ich freue mich darauf, Sie wiederzusehen.
Best wishes	Schöne Grüße
shop assistant	Verkäufer/in
God	Gott

Unit 5

instructions	Anweisungen
copier/copying machine	Kopierer
green	grün
light	Licht
on	an
Oh dear!	O je!
We must tell John.	Wir müssen es John sagen.
plug	Stecker
socket	Steckdose
plug in (v)	einstecken
switch on (v)	anschalten
press (v)	drücken
switch	Schalter
on the left	links
button	Knopf
warm up (v)	aufwärmen
bring (v)	bringen
print (v)	drucken
envelope	Briefumschlag
Post Office	Postamt
forget (v)	vergessen
ask for (something) (v)	um etwas bitten
receipt	Quittung
before you get there	bevor Sie dort ankommen
Excuse me!	Entschuldigung!
Can you tell me the way to the Post Office?	Können Sie mir sagen, wie ich zum Postamt komme?
go out	gehen Sie hinaus
door	Tür
turn right (v)	rechts abbiegen/biegen Sie rechts ab
second	zweite/r
Take the second turning on the left.	Nehmen Sie die zweite Straße links.
traffic lights	Ampel
cross the road (v)	die Straße überqueren
go straight ahead (v)	geradeaus weiter-fahren/weitergehen
follow (v)	folgen
railway bridge	Bahnbrücke
main road	Hauptstraße
past	vorbei
crossroads	Kreuzung
motorway	Autobahn
direction	Richtung
appointment	Termin
someone	jemand
take a seat (v)	sich setzen
seat	Sitzplatz
electricity	Elektrizität
electricity company	Stromversorger
company identity card	Firmenausweis
lift	Aufzug
floor	Stock
spell (v)	buchstabieren
minus	minus
dot	Punkt

letter	Buchstabe
sounds like	hört sich an wie
article	Artikel
slash	Schrägstrich
underline (v)	unterstreichen
underscore	Unterstrich
dot	Punkt
brackets	Klammern
dash	Strich
inverted commas	Anführungsstriche
italics	Kursivschrift
bold	fett (Schrift)
capital letter	Großbuchstabe
article	Artikel
January	Januar
February	Februar
March	März
April	April
May	Mai
June	Juni
July	Juli
August	August
September	September
October	Oktober
November	November
December	Dezember
Mother's day	Muttertag
public holiday	öffentlicher Feiertag
Christmas eve	Heiliger Abend
Christmas day	Dezember 25th
New Year's day	1. Januar
New Year's eve	Silvester
independence	Unabhängigkeit
nowhere else	nirgendwo sonst
alone	allein
leap year	Schaltjahr
calendar	Kalender
both	beide
free dinner	kostenloses Abendessen
hope (v)	hoffen
let me know	lassen Sie es mich wissen
know (v)	wissen
order	Reihenfolge
I was born	Ich wurde geboren
flower	Blume

Unit 6

like (v)	mögen
hate (v)	hassen
never mind	es macht nichts
What about music?	Was ist mit Musik?
Angel	Engel
love	Liebe
same	selbe/r
food	Essen
love (v)	lieben
That is a start!	Das ist ein Anfang!
factory	Fabrik
ice-cream	(Speise-)Eis
not … at all	gar nicht …
receptionist	Empfangssekretärin
visitor	Besucher/in
visit (v)	besuchen
person	Person
enter data (v)	Daten eingeben
get up (v)	aufstehen
then	dann
have a shower (v)	sich duschen
drink (v)	trinken
eat (v)	essen
coffee break	Kaffeepause
finish work (v)	Feierabend haben
usually	gewöhnlich
after	nach
I go home.	Ich gehe nach Hause.
glass	Glas
wine	Wein
never	nie
seldom	selten
always	immer
normally	normalerweise
fast	schnell
Switzerland	Schweiz
Italy	Italien
every evening	jeden Abend

newspaper	Zeitung
smoke (v)	rauchen
bottle	Flasche
early	früh
Do you take milk?	Nehmen Sie Milch?
Here you are.	Hier, bitte.
lovely	sehr schön
think (v)	denken
often	oft
summer	Sommer
go for walks (v)	Spaziergänge machen
which	welche
form	Schulklasse
chat (v)	plaudern
each other	einander
typical	typisch
watch the news (v)	die Nachrichten schauen
room (= hotel room)	Zimmer
you are lucky	Sie haben Glück
double room	Doppelzimmer
single room	Einzelzimmer
all week	für die ganze Woche
book (v)	buchen
night	Nacht
bathroom	Badezimmer
toilet	Toilette
television	Fernseher
per night	pro Nacht
jam	Marmelade
included	im Preis
egg	Ei
bacon	Schinken
reserve (v)	reservieren
fly (v)	fliegen
seldom	selten
personal	persönlich
take (v)	nehmen

Unit 7

routine	Routine
plane	Flugzeug
on a plane	in einem Flugzeug
air steward	Flugbegleiter
Irish	irisch
airline	Fluglinie
passenger	Passagier
boarding card	Bordkarte
welcome (v)	willkommen heißen
emergency	Notfall
fasten one's seatbelt	anschnallen
seat belt	Sicherheitsgurt
air	Luft
perfume	Parfüm
travel (v)	reisen
different	verschieden
country	Land
safe	sicher
not … either	auch nicht …
free time	Freizeit
pilot	Pilot
licence	Lizenz
passenger plane	Passagierflugzeug
garden	Garten
sell (v)	verkaufen
cigars	Zigarren
play the guitar (v)	Gitarre spielen
chocolate	Schokolade
aunt	Tante
still	immer noch
writer	Schriftsteller(in)
grandchild	Enkelkind
uncle	Onkel
dead	tot
alone	allein
dog	Hund
pet	Haustier
printer	Drucker
cost (v)	kosten
full	voll
guarantee	Garantie
ink	Tinte
use (v)	verbrauchen
less	weniger
figure	Zahl
discount	Rabatt

order	Bestellung
My PC doesn't work.	Mein PC funktioniert nicht.
customer number	Kundennummer
nothing	nichts
course	Kurs
beginner	Anfänger
register (v)	sich anmelden
second-hand	gebraucht
old	alt
gear	Gang
brake	Bremse
work	funktionieren
enquiry	Anfrage
look for (v)	suchen
enclosed	beigefügt
catalogue	Katalog
reply	Antwort
specifications	detaillierte Angaben
detailed	detailliert
We look forward to hearing from you.	Wir freuen uns auf ihre Antwort.
offer	Angebot
hesitate (v)	zögern
Do not hesitate to contact us.	Zögern Sie nicht, sich mit uns in Verbindung zu setzen.
order	Bestellung
kiss	Kuss
first-hand	neu
third class	drittklassig

Unit 8

brown	braun
was	war
were	waren
yesterday	gestern
the day before yesterday	vorgestern
last weekend	letztes Wochenende
sunny	sonnig
until	bis
earn (v)	verdienen
Greek	griechisch
need (v)	brauchen/benötigen
file	Datei
half an hour ago	vor einer halben Stunde
take place (v)	stattfinden
tell (v)	sagen/informieren
guest	Gast
guest family	Gastfamilie
payment	Bezahlung
luggage	Gepäck
weight	Gewicht
weight limit	Höchstgewicht
case	Koffer

Vokabelverzeichnis – Englisch/Deutsch

a little bit	ein bisschen
a little	ein bisschen
a lot of	eine Menge/viele
a lot to do	eine Menge zu tun
a/an	ein
about	über/wegen
account	Konto
accountant	Buchhalter/in
actor	Schauspieler
actress	Schauspielerin
address	Adresse
after	nach
agenda	Tagesordnung
air steward	Flugbegleiter
air	Luft
airline	Fluglinie
airport	Flughafen
all week	für die ganze Woche
alone	allein
always	immer
American	amerikanisch
Angel	Engel
Ann speaking	Ann am Apparat
another call	noch ein Anruf
answer (v)	antworten/beantworten
answer the phone	ein Gespräch annehmen
apologise (v)	sich entschuldigen
apple juice	Apfelsaft
apple pie	Apfeltasche
appointment	Termin
April	April
are	sind
arrive (v)	ankommen
article	Artikel
as … as	so … wie
as soon as possible	so schnell wie möglich
asap	so bald wie möglich
ask (v)	fragen
ask for (something) (v)	um etwas bitten
assistant	Assistent/in
attached file/ attachment	Anhang (bei Briefen und E-Mails)
August	August
aunt	Tante
available	erreichbar
back	zurück/Rückseite
bacon	Schinken
bag	Tasche
bank clerk	Bankangestellte/r
bank	Bank
bathroom	Badezimmer
be (v)	sein
before	vor
beginner	Anfänger
beside	neben
Best regards	Mit freundlichen Grüßen
Best wishes	Schöne Grüße
better	besser
big	groß
birthday	Geburtstag
biscuits	Kekse
black	schwarz
blue	blau
boarding card	Bordkarte
bold	fett (Schrift)
book (v)	buchen
book	Buch
boss	Chef/in
both	beide
bottle	Flasche
boy	Junge
brackets	Klammern
brake	Bremse
bread	Brot
breakfast	Frühstück
bridge	Brücke
bring (v)	bringen
British	britisch
brother	Bruder
brown	braun
bus station	Busbahnhof
bus	Bus
business trip	Geschäftsreise

business	Geschäft
bus-stop	Bushaltestelle
busy	beschäftigt
but	aber
button	Knopf
buy (v)	kaufen
café	Café
cake	Kuchen
calendar	Kalender
(phone) call	Anruf
call (v)	anrufen
call back (v)	zurückrufen
call	Anruf
caller	Anrufer
can (v)	können
canteer	Kantine
capital letter	Großbuchstabe
car	Auto
case	Koffer
catalogue	Katalog
chain	Kette
chair	Stuhl
change	Kleingeld
chat (v)	plaudern
cheap	billig
check (v)	überprüfen
Cheerio!	Tschüss!
chicken	Huhn
child/children	Kind/Kinder
chips	Pommes
chocolate	Schokolade
Christmas day	Dezember 25th
Christmas eve	Heiliger Abend
church	Kirche
cigars	Zigarren
cinema	Kino
city centre	Stadtzentrum
city	Stadt
class	Klasse
classroom	Klassenzimmer
clock	Uhr
coffee break	Kaffeepause
coffee-bar	Café
collect (v)	abholen
come (v)	kommen
company identity card	Firmenausweis
company	Gesellschaft
complete (v)	ergänzen
concert hall	Konzerthalle
confirm (v)	bestätigen
contact	Kontakt
cook (v)	kochen
copier/copying machine	Kopierer
copy (v)	kopieren
correct	korrekt, richtig
correct (v)	korrigieren
corrected	korrigiert
cost (v)	kosten
country	Land
course	Kurs
cousin	Vetter/Kusine
crisps	Chips
crossroads	Kreuzung
cup of coffee	Tasse Kaffee
cup	Tasse
customer number	Kundennummer
customer	Kunde/Kundin
dance (v)	tanzen
dash	Strich
date of birth	Geburtsdatum
date	Datum
date	Rendezvous
day	Tag
dead	tot
December	Dezember
department store	Warenhaus
design department	Designabteilung
desk	Schreibtisch
dessert	Nachtisch/Nachspeise
detailed	detailliert
dial (v)	wählen (Telefon)
dialling code	Vorwahl
different	verschieden
dinner	Abendessen
direction	Richtung
director	Direktor/in

discount	Rabatt
discuss (v)	besprechen
divorced	geschieden
do (v)	tun/machen
Do you want to hold on?	Wollen Sie warten?
doctor	Arzt/Ärztin
dog	Hund
door	Tür
dot	Punkt
double room	Doppelzimmer
drink (v)	trinken
drinks	Getränke
driver	Fahrer/in
each other	einander
early	früh
earn (v)	verdienen
eat (v)	essen
egg	Ei
electricity company	Stromversorger
electricity	Elektrizität
emergency	Notfall
employee	Angestellte/r
enclosed	beigefügt
end	Ende
English	englisch
enquiry	Anfrage
enter data (v)	Daten eingeben
envelope	Briefumschlag
evening	Abend
every day	jeden Tag
Excuse me!	Entschuldigung!
expensive	teuer
extension number	Durchwahl
eye	Auge
factory	Fabrik
family name/last name/ surname	Familienname/ Nachname
fast	schnell
fasten one's seatbelt	anschnallen (sich)
father	Vater
favourite singer	Lieblingssänger/-in
favourite	Lieblings-
February	Februar
figure	Zahl
file	Datei
fill in (v)	ausfüllen
film	Film
finance department	Finanzabteilung
find (v)	finden
finish work (v)	Feierabend haben
firm	Firma
first	erst
first-hand	neu
fish	Fisch
flag	Fahne
flat	Wohnung
flight number	Flugnummer
flight	Flug
floor	Stock
flower	Blume
fluently	fließend
fly (v)	fliegen
follow (v)	folgen
food	Essen
football	Fußball
for example	zum Beispiel
forename/first name	Vorname
forget (v)	vergessen
form	Formular/Schulklasse
free dinner	kostenloses Abendessen
free time	Freizeit
free	frei
French	französisch
fried	gebraten
friend	Freund/in
from … to	von … bis
from	von/aus
full	voll
garden	Garten
gear	Gang
German	deutsch
Germany	Deutschland
get (v)	bekommen
get home (v)	zu Hause ankommen
get up (v)	aufstehen
girl	Mädchen
give (v)	geben

Give ... my love.	Viele Grüße an ...
Give my regards to ...	Grüß(en Sie) ... von mir.
glass	Glas
go for walks (v)	Spaziergänge machen
go out	gehen Sie hinaus
goalkeeper	Torhüter
God	Gott
Good afternoon	Guten Tag
good	gut
Goodbye/Bye	Auf Wiedersehen/ Auf Wiederhören
grandchild	Enkelkind
grandmother	Großmutter
Greek	griechisch
green	grün
grey	grau
group	Gruppe
guarantee	Garantie
guest family	Gastfamilie
guest	Gast
guy (slang)	Typ/Kollege
hair	Haare
half an hour ago	vor einer halben Stunde
half	halb
ham	Schinken
happy	glücklich
hard	schwer
hate (v)	hassen
have (v)	haben
Have a nice day!	Schönen Tag noch!
have fun (v)	Spaß haben
he	er
head of department	Abteilungsleiter/in
head office	Hauptbüro
her	ihr/e
Here you are.	Hier, bitte.
here	hier
hesitate (v)	zögern
his	sein/e
hobby	Hobby
holiday	Urlaub/Ferien
home town	Heimatort
hope (v)	hoffen
horse	Pferd

hot	heiß
house	Haus
How are you?	Wie geht es Ihnen? Wie geht es dir/euch?
How can I help you?	Wie kann ich Ihnen helf-en?
How do you do?	Erfreut, Sie kennenzu-lernen.
how	wie
hungry	hungrig
hurry (v)	sich beeilen
husband	Ehemann
I was born	Ich wurde geboren
I will (I'll)	ich werde
I wish you were here!	Ich wünschte, du wärst hier!
I	ich
I'm (I am)	ich bin
I'm fine.	Mir geht es gut.
I'm looking forward to it.	Ich freue mich darauf.
ice-cream	(Speise-)Eis
if	falls
important	wichtig
in a few minutes	in einigen Minuten
in the office	im Büro
included	im Preis
incorrect	falsch, fehlerhaft
independence	Unabhängigkeit
information	Information
ink	Tinte
instructions	Anweisungen
interesting	interessant
interpreter	Dolmetscher/in
Introduce yourself.	Stellen Sie sich vor.
inverted commas	Anführungsstriche
invitation	Einladung
invoice	Rechnung
Irish	irisch
is	ist
it	es
Italian	italienisch
italics	Kursivschrift
Italy	Italien
jam	Marmelade

January	Januar
Japanese	japanisch
job	Arbeit/Aufgabe
journey	Reise
July	Juli
June	Juni
key	Taste (am Computer); Schlüssel
kind	nett
kiss	Kuss
know (v)	wissen
lamp	Lampe
last weekend	letztes Wochenende
late	spät
later	später
leap year	Schaltjahr
learn (v)	lernen
Learning by playing	Lernen durch Spielen
leave home (v)	das Haus verlassen
less	weniger
lesson	Klassenstunde
Let's go!	Gehen wir!
letter	Brief/Buchstabe
letter-post	Briefpost
licence	Lizenz
lift	Aufzug
light	Licht
like (v)	mögen
like	so wie
listen to (v)	zuhören
little	klein
long	lange
look for (v)	suchen
Look!	Schauen Sie! Guck mal!
lottery	Lotto
love	Liebe
love (v)	lieben
lovely	sehr schön
luggage	Gepäck
lunch break	Mittagspause
lunch	Mittagessen
magazine	Illustrierte
main dish	Hauptgericht
main road	Hauptstraße

make (v)	machen
man/men	Mann/Männer
managing director	Geschäftsführer
March	März
marital status	Familienstand
market place	Marktplatz
married	verheiratet
match	Spiel
May	Mai
mean (v)	bedeuten
mechanic	Mechaniker/in
meet (v)	kennenlernen
meet (v)	treffen
meeting	Besprechung
member	Mitglied
menu	Speisekarte
message	Nachricht, Mitteilung
milk	Milch
mineral water	Mineralwasser
mint	Minze
minus	minus
minutes	Protokoll
mistake	Fehler
mobile (phone) number	Handynummer
mobile phone	Handy
Monday	Montag
money	Geld
morning	Morgen/Vormittag
mother	Mutter
Mother's day	Muttertag
motorway	Autobahn
mouse/mice	Maus/Mäuse
must (v)	müssen
my	mein/e
name	Name
nationality	Nationalität
near	in der Nähe von
need (v)	brauchen/benötigen
never mind	es macht nichts
never	nie
New Year's day	1. Januar
New Year's eve	Silvester
new	neu

newspaper	Zeitung
next	nächste
nice	schön/nett
night	Nacht
normally	normalerweise
North	Norden
not … at all	gar nicht …
not … either	auch nicht …
note	Geldschein
nothing	nichts
November	November
Now you talk!	Jetzt reden Sie!
now	jetzt
nowhere else	nirgendwo sonst
number	Nummer
occupation	Beruf
October	Oktober
of course	natürlich
offer	Angebot
office worker	Büroarbeiter/in
office	Büro
often	oft
Oh dear!	O je!
old	alt
on	an/auf
one moment	einen Moment
only	nur
open	offen
order	Bestellung
order number	Bestellnummer
order	Reihenfolge
our	unser
out of order	außer Betrieb
oxtail	Ochsenschwanz
pardon?	Wie bitte?
park	Park
partner	Partner/Partnerin
passenger plane	Passagierflugzeug
passenger	Passagier
past	nach/vorbei
pay (v)	bezahlen
payment	Bezahlung
peas	Erbsen
per night	pro Nacht
perfume	Parfüm
person	Person
personal	persönlich
pet	Haustier
phone (v)	telefonieren
photo/photograph	Foto
piano	Klavier
picture	Bild
piece	Scheibe
pilot	Pilot
place of birth	Geburtsort
plane	Flugzeug
play (v)	spielen
player	Spieler/in
Please hold the line.	Bitte warten Sie.
please	bitte
Pleased to meet you.	Erfreut, Sie kennenzulernen.
plug in (v)	einstecken
plug	Stecker
plural	Mehrzahl
pocket	Tasche
possible	möglich
Post Office	Postamt
postal code	Postleitzahl
pot	Kanne
potato	Kartoffel
pound	Pfund (britische Währung)
prepare (v)	vorbereiten
press (v)	drücken
pretty	hübsch
price	Preis
print (v)	drucken
printer	Drucker
problem	Problem
professor	Professor/in
programmer	Programmierer/in
project	Projekt
pub	Kneipe
public holiday	öffentlicher Feiertag
Put me through.	Stellen Sie mich durch.
quarter	Viertel

queen	Königin
question	Frage
racing driver	Rennfahrer/in
railway bridge	Bahnbrücke
railway company	Bahngesellschaft
railway station	Bahnhof
rain (v)	regnen
reach (v)	erreichen
read (v)	lesen
really	wirklich
receipt	Quittung
receive	bekommen
reception	Rezeption/Empfang
receptionist	Empfangssekretärin
recipient	Empfänger
red	rot
register (v)	sich anmelden
relax (v)	sich entspannen
repair (v)	reparieren
repeat	wiederholen
reply	Antwort
report	Bericht
reserve (v)	reservieren
restaurant	Restaurant
return (ticket)	Hin- und Rückfahrkarte
ride (v)	reiten
right	richtig
ring (v)	klingeln
river	Fluss
roast lamb	Lammbraten
roast potato	Röstkartoffel
room (= hotel room)	Zimmer
room	Raum
routine	Routine
rugby	Rugby
rule	Regel
run (v)	laufen
safe	sicher
sail (v)	segeln
salad	Salat
sale	Verkauf
sales department	Verkaufsabteilung
sales director	Verkaufsdirektor/in
salesman	Verkäufer
saleswoman	Verkäuferin
same	selbe/r
sand-castle	Sandburg
sandwich	belegtes Brot
Saturday	Samstag
sauce	Soße
sausage	Wurst
say (v)	sagen
sea	Meer
seat belt	Sicherheitsgurt
seat	Sitzplatz
second	zweite/r
second-hand	gebraucht
secretary	Sekretär/in
see (v)	sehen
See you later!	Bis später!
See you soon.	Bis bald.
See you.	Wir sehen uns.
seldom	selten
seldom	selten
sell (v)	verkaufen
send (v)	schicken
sender	Absender
sentence	Satz
September	September
she	sie
shine (v)	scheinen
shop assistant	Verkäufer/in
shop	Geschäft
shopping centre	Einkaufszentrum
signature	Unterschrift
similar	ähnlich
sing (v)	singen
singer	Sänger/in
single (ticket)	Einzelfahrschein
single room	Einzelzimmer
single	ledig
sit (v)	sitzen
ski (v)	Skifahren
sky	Himmel
slash	Schrägstrich
sleep (v)	schlafen

slowly	langsam
small	klein
smoke (v)	rauchen
snow (v)	schneien
soccer	Fußball
socket	Steckdose
some	einige
someone	jemand
son	Sohn
sorry	es tut mir leid
sounds like	hört sich an wie
soup	Suppe
speak (v)	sprechen
specifications	detaillierte Angaben
spell (v)	buchstabieren
sports ground	Sportplatz
sportsman	Sportler
sportswoman	Sportlerin
stadium	Stadion
starter	Vorspeise
stay (v)	bleiben
still	immer noch
stone	Stein
stop (v)	anhalten
stress	Stress
student	Student/in
subject	Betreff
sugar	Zucker
summer	Sommer
sun	Sonne
sunbathe (v)	sich sonnen
Sunday	Sonntag
sunny	sonnig
supermarket	Supermarkt
sure	sicher
swim (v)	schwimmen
switch on (v)	anschalten
switch	Schalter
Switzerland	Schweiz
table	Tisch
take (v)	nehmen
take a seat (v)	sich setzen
take place (v)	stattfinden

talk (v)	reden
tea	Tee
teacher	Lehrer/in
team	Mannschaft
technician	Techniker/in
telephone message	Telefonnachricht
television	Fernseher
tell (v)	sagen/informieren
text	Text
thanks	Danke
that	dass
That's a pity!	Schade!
the day before yesterday	vorgestern
the	der/die/das
theatre	Theater
their	ihr/e
then	dann
There is no answer.	Es geht niemand ans Telefon.
there is/there are	es gibt
they	sie (Mehrzahl)
thing	Ding
think (v)	denken
third class	drittklassig
thirsty	durstig
this afternoon	heute Nachmittag
this	dies
Thursday	Donnerstag
ticket	Fahrkarte
time	Uhrzeit/Zeit
timetable	Fahrplan
tip	Tipp
today	heute
toilet	Toilette
tomato	Tomate
tomorrow	morgen
too many	zu viele
too	auch
town	Stadt
traffic lights	Ampel
trainee	Auszubildende/r, Praktikant/in
transfer (v)	überweisen

translate	übersetzen
translator	Übersetzer/in
travel (v)	reisen
try (v)	versuchen
try later (v)	(es) später versuchen
Tuesday	Dienstag
turn right (v)	rechts abbiegen/ biegen Sie rechts ab
type (v)	tippen
typical	typisch
uncle	Onkel
underline (v)	unterstreichen
underscore	Unterstrich
understand	verstehen
university	Universität
until	bis
use (v)	verbrauchen
usually	gewöhnlich
very	sehr
village	Dorf
visit (v)	besuchen
visitor	Besucher/in
vote (v)	wählen
wait (v)	warten
waiter	Kellner
waitress	Kellnerin
walk (v)	laufen/spazieren
wall	Wand
warm up (v)	aufwärmen
warm	warm
was	war
watch (v)	zuschauen
watch TV (v)	fernsehen
watch	(Armband-)Uhr
water filter	Wasserfilter
water	Wasser
way	Weg
we	wir
Wednesday	Mittwoch
week	Woche
weekend	Wochenende
weight limit	Höchstgewicht
weight	Gewicht
welcome (v)	willkommen heißen
well	gut
were	waren
What about music?	Was ist mit Musik?
What is ... like?	Wie ist ...?
What is the time?	Wie spät ist es?
what?	was?
When can I reach him?	Wann kann ich ihn erreichen?
where	wo
which	welche
white	weiß
who	wer
wife	Ehefrau
win (v)	gewinnen
window	Fenster
wine	Wein
winter	Winter
with	mit
woman/women	Frau/Frauen
won't (will not)	werden nicht
work (v)	arbeiten
work	Arbeit
work (v)	funktionieren
world cup	Weltmeisterschaft
write (v)	schreiben
writer	Schriftsteller(in)
wrong	falsch
year	Jahr
yellow	gelb
yesterday	gestern
you are lucky	Sie haben Glück
You are welcome!	Bitte/Gern geschehen!
your	dein/e, euer, eure, Ihr/e
youth club	Jugendzentrum

Vokabelverzeichnis – Deutsch/Englisch

Armbanduhr	watch
später versuchen	try later (v)
(Speise-)Eis	ice-cream
1. Januar	New Year's day
12 Uhr mittags	high noon
Abend	evening
Abendessen	Dinner
aber	but
abholen	collect (v)
Absender	sender
Abteilungsleiter/in	head of department
Adresse	address
ähnlich	similar
allein	alone
alt	old
amerikanisch	American
Ampel	traffic lights
an	on
Anfänger	beginner
Anfrage	enquiry
Anführungsstriche	inverted commas
Angebot	offer
Angestellte/r	employee
anhalten	stop (v)
Anhang (bei Briefen und E-Mails)	attached file/ attachment
ankommen	arrive (v)
Anruf	call
anrufen	call (v)
Anrufer	caller
anschalten	switch on (v)
anschnallen (sich)	fasten one's seatbelt
Antwort	reply
antworten/beantworten	answer (v)
Anweisungen	instructions
Apfelsaft	apple juice
Apfeltasche	apple pie
April	April
Arbeit	work
Arbeit/Aufgabe	job
arbeiten	work (v)
Artikel	article
Arzt/Ärztin	doctor
Assistent/in	assistant
auch nicht …	not … either
auch	too
auf dem Weg nach	on the way to
Auf Wiedersehen/ Auf Wiederhören	Goodbye/Bye
auf	on
aufstehen	get up (v)
aufwärmen	warm up (v)
Aufzug	lift
Auge	eye
August	August
ausfüllen	fill in (v)
außer Betrieb	out of order
Auszubildende/r, Praktikant/in	trainee
Auto	car
Autobahn	motorway
Badezimmer	bathroom
Bahnbrücke	railway bridge
Bahngesellschaft	railway company
Bahnhof	railway station
Bank	bank
Bankangestellte/r	bank clerk
bedeuten	mean (v)
beide	both
beigefügt	enclosed
bekommen	get (v)/receive
belegtes Brot	sandwich
Bericht	report
Beruf	occupation
beschäftigt	busy
besprechen	discuss (v)
Besprechung	meeting
besser	better
bestätigen	confirm (v)
Bestellnummer	order number
Bestellung	order
besuchen	visit (v)
Besucher/in	visitor
Betreff	subject

bezahlen	pay (v)
Bezahlung	payment
Bild	picture
billig	cheap
Bis bald.	See you soon.
Bis später!	See you later!
bis	until
Bitte warten Sie.	Please hold the line.
bitte	please
Bitte/Gern geschehen!	You are welcome!
blau	blue
bleiben	stay (v)
Blume	flower
Bordkarte	boarding card
brauchen/benötigen	need (v)
braun	brown
Bremse	brake
Brief	letter
Briefpost	letter-post
Briefumschlag	envelope
bringen	bring (v)
britisch	British
Brot	bread
Brücke	bridge
Bruder	brother
Buch	book
buchen	book (v)
Buchhalter/in	accountant
Buchstabe	letter
buchstabieren	spell (v)
Büro	office
Büroarbeiter/in	office worker
Bus	bus
Busbahnhof	bus station
Bushaltestelle	bus-stop
Café	café/coffee-bar
Chef/in	boss
Chips	crisps
Danke	thanks
dann	then
das Haus verlassen	leave home (v)
dass	that
Datei	file
Daten eingeben	enter data (v)

Datum	date
dein/e, euer, eure, Ihr/e	your
denken	think (v)
der/die/das	the
Designabteilung	design department
detailliert	detailed
detaillierte Angaben	specifications
deutsch	German
Deutschland	Germany
Dezember 25th	Christmas day
Dezember	December
Die Leitung ist besetzt.	The line is busy.
die Straße überqueren	cross the road (v)
Dienstag	Tuesday
dies	this
Ding	thing
Direktor/in	director
Dolmetscher/in	interpreter
Donnerstag	Thursday
Doppelzimmer	double room
Dorf	village
drittklassig	third class
drücken	press (v)
drucken	print (v)
Drucker	printer
Durchwahl	extension number
durstig	thirsty
Ehefrau	wife
Ehemann	husband
Ei	egg
ein bisschen	a little (bit)
ein Gespräch annehmen	answer the phone
ein Treffen vereinbaren	arrange (v) a meeting
ein	a/an
einander	each other
eine Liste	a list
eine Menge/viele	a lot of
einen Moment	one moment
einige	some
Einkaufszentrum	shopping centre
Einladung	invitation
einstecken	plug in (v)
Einzelfahrschein	single (ticket)
Einzelzimmer	single room

Eis	ice cream
Elektrizität	electricity
Empfänger	recipient
Empfangssekretärin	receptionist
Ende	end
Engel	Angel
englisch	English
Enkelkind	grandchild
Entschuldigung!	Excuse me!
er	he
Erbsen	peas
Erfreut, Sie kennenzulernen.	How do you do?/Pleased to meet you.
ergänzen	complete (v)
erreichbar	available
erreichen	reach (v)
erst	first
Es geht niemand ans Telefon.	There is no answer.
es gibt	there is/there are
es macht nichts	never mind
es tut mir leid	sorry
es	it
essen	eat (v)
Essen	food
Fabrik	factory
Fahne	flag
Fahrer/in	driver
Fahrkarte	ticket
Fahrplan	timetable
falls	if
falsch	wrong/incorrect
falsch, fehlerhaft	incorrect
Familienname/ Nachname	family name/last name/ surname
Familienstand	marital status
Februar	February
Fehler	mistake
Feierabend haben	finish work (v)
Fenster	window
fernsehen	watch TV (v)
Fernseher	television
fett (Schrift)	bold
Film	film
Finanzabteilung	finance department
finden	find (v)
Firma	firm
Firmenausweis	company identity card
Fisch	fish
Flasche	bottle
fliegen	fly (v)
fließend	fluently
Flug	flight
Flugbegleiter	air steward
Flughafen	airport
Fluglinie	airline
Flugnummer	flight number
Flugzeug	plane
Fluss	river
folgen	follow (v)
Formular	form
Foto	photo/photograph
Frage	question
fragen	ask (v)
französisch	French
Frau/Frauen	woman/women
frei	free
Freizeit	free time
Freund/in	friend
früh	early
Frühstück	breakfast
funktionieren	work
für Freitag	for Friday
Fußball	football/soccer
Gang	gear
gar nicht …	not … at all
Garantie	guarantee
Garten	garden
Gast	guest
Gastfamilie	guest family
geben	give (v)
gebraten	fried
gebraucht	second-hand
Geburtsdatum	date of birth
Geburtsort	place of birth
Geburtstag	birthday
Gehen wir!	Let's go!
gelb	yellow
Geld	money

Geldschein	note
Gepäck	luggage
geradeaus weiter-fahren/weitergehen	go straight ahead (v)
Geschäft	business/shop
Geschäftsführer	managing director
Geschäftsreise	business trip
geschieden	divorced
Gesellschaft	company
gestern	yesterday
Getränke	drinks
Gewicht	weight
gewinnen	win (v)
gewöhnlich	usually
Glas	glass
glücklich	happy
Gott	God
grau	grey
griechisch	Greek
groß	big
Großbuchstaben	capital letters
Großmutter	grandmother
grün	green
Gruppe	group
Grüß(en Sie) … von mir.	Give my regards to …
gut	good
gut	well
Guten Tag	Good afternoon
Haare	hair
haben	have (v)
halb	half
Handy	mobile phone
Handynummer	mobile (phone) number
hassen	hate (v)
Hauptbüro	head office
Hauptgericht	main dish
Hauptstraße	main road
Haus	house
Haustier	pet
Heiliger Abend	Christmas eve
Heimatort	home town
heiß	hot
heute Nachmittag	this afternoon
heute	today
hier	here
Hier, bitte.	Here you are.
Himmel	sky
Hin- und Rückfahrkarte	return (ticket)
Hobby	hobby
Höchstgewicht	weight limit
hoffen	hope (v)
hört sich an wie	sounds like
hübsch	pretty
Huhn	chicken
Hund	dog
hungrig	hungry
Ich freue mich darauf, Sie wiederzusehen.	I look forward to meeting you again.
Ich freue mich darauf.	I'm looking forward to it.
Ich gehe nach Hause.	I go home.
ich verbinde	I'll connect you
ich werde	I will (I'll)
Ich will/möchte	I want to
Ich wünschte, du wärst hier!	I wish you were here!
Ich wurde geboren	I was born
ich	I
ihr/e	her
ihr/e	their
Illustrierte	magazine
im Preis	included
immer noch	still
immer	always
in der Nähe von	near
in der Schule	at school
in einem Flugzeug	on a plane
in einigen Minuten	in a few minutes
in Urlaub	on holiday
Information	information
interessant	interesting
irisch	Irish
ist	is
Italien	Italy
italienisch	Italian
Jahr	year
Januar	January
japanisch	Japanese

jeden Tag	every day
jemand	someone
Jetzt reden Sie!	Now you talk!
jetzt	now
Jugendzentrum	youth club
Juli	July
Junge	boy
Juni	June
Kaffeepause	coffee break
Kalender	calendar
Kanne	pot
Kantine	canteen
Kartoffel	potato
Katalog	catalogue
kaufen (v)	buy
Kekse	biscuits
Kellner/Kellnerin	waiter/waitress
kennenlernen	meet (v)
Kette	chain
Kind/Kinder	child/children
Kino	cinema
Kirche	church
Klammern	brackets
Klasse	class
Klassenstunde	lesson
Klassenzimmer	classroom
Klavier	piano
klein	little/small
Kleingeld	change
klingeln	ring (v)
Kneipe	pub
Knopf	button
kochen	cook (v)
Koffer	case
kommen	come (v)
Königin	queen
können	can (v)
Kontakt	contact
Konto	account
Konzerthalle	concert hall
kopieren	copy (v)
Kopierer	copier/copying machine
korrekt, richtig	correct
korrigieren	correct

korrigiert	corrected
kosten	cost (v)
Kreuzung	crossroads
Kuchen	cake
Kunde/Kundin	customer
Kundennummer	customer number
Kurs	course
Kursivschrift	italics
Kuss	kiss
Lammbraten	roast lamb
Lampe	lamp
Land	country
lange	long
langsam	slowly
lassen Sie es mich wissen	let me know
laufen	run (v)
laufen/spazieren	walk (v)
ledig	single
Lehrer/in	teacher
Lernen durch Spielen	Learning by playing
lernen	learn (v)
lesen	read (v)
letztes Wochenende	last weekend
Licht	light
Liebe	love
lieben	love (v)
Lieblings-	favourite
Lieblingssänger/-in	favourite singer
links	on the left
Lizenz	licence
Lotto	lottery
Luft	air
machen	make (v)
Mädchen	girl
Mai	May
Mann/Männer	man/men
Mannschaft	team
Marktplatz	market place
Marmelade	jam
März	March
Maus/Mäuse	mouse/mice
Mechaniker/in	mechanic
Meer	sea

Mehrzahl	plural
mein/e	my
Milch	milk
Mineralwasser	mineral water
minus	minus
Minze	mint
Mir geht es gut.	I'm fine.
mit der Post	by letter-post
Mit freundlichen Grüßen	Best regards
mit	with
Mitglied	member
Mittagessen	lunch
Mittagspause	lunch break
Mittwoch	Wednesday
mögen	like (v)
möglich	possible
Montag	Monday
morgen	tomorrow
Morgen/Vormittag	morning
müssen	must (v)
Mutter	mother
Muttertag	Mother's day
nach	after
nach	past
Nachricht/Mitteilung	message
nächste	next
Nacht	night
Nachtisch/Nachspeise	dessert
Name	name
Nationalität	nationality
natürlich	of course
neben	beside
nehmen	take (v)
nett	kind
neu	first-hand
neu	new
nichts	nothing
nie	never
nirgendwo sonst	nowhere else
noch ein Anruf	another call
Norden	North
normalerweise	normally
Notfall	emergency
notiert von	taken by
November	November
Nummer	number
nur	only
O je!	Oh dear!
Ochsenschwanz	oxtail
offen	open
öffentlicher Feiertag	public holiday
oft	often
Oktober	October
Onkel	uncle
Parfüm	perfume
Park	park
Partner/Partnerin	partner
Passagier	passenger
Passagierflugzeug	passenger plane
Person	person
persönlich	personal
Pferd	horse
Pfund	pound
Pilot	pilot
plaudern	chat (v)
Pommes	chips
Postamt	Post Office
Postleitzahl	postal code
Preis	price
pro Nacht	per night
Problem	problem
Professor/in	professor
Programmierer/in	programmer
Projekt	project
Protokoll	minutes
Punkt	dot
Punkt	dot
Quittung	receipt
Rabatt	discount
rauchen	smoke (v)
Raum	room
Rechnung	invoice
rechts abbiegen	turn right (v)
reden	talk (v)
Regel	rule
regnen	rain (v)

Reihenfolge	order
Reise	journey
reisen	travel (v)
reiten	ride (v)
Rendezvous	date
Rennfahrer/in	racing driver
reparieren	repair (v)
reservieren	reserve (v)
Restaurant	restaurant
Rezeption/Empfang	reception
richtig	right
Richtung	direction
Röstkartoffel	roast potato
rot	red
Routine	routine
Rugby	rugby
sagen	say (v)
sagen/informieren	tell (v)
Salat	salad
Samstag	Saturday
Sandburg	sand-castle
Sänger/in	singer
Satz	sentence
Schade!	That's a pity!
Schalter	switch
Schaltjahr	leap year
Schauen Sie! Guck mal!	Look!
Schauspieler	actor
Schauspielerin	actress
Scheibe	piece
scheinen	shine (v)
schicken	send (v)
Schinken	ham
schlafen	sleep
schneien	snow (v)
schnell	fast
Schokolade	chocolate
schön/nett	nice
Schöne Grüße	Best wishes
Schönen Tag noch!	Have a nice day!
Schrägstrich	slash
schreiben	write (v)
Schreibtisch	desk
Schriftsteller(in)	writer
Schulklasse	form
schwarz	black
Schweiz	Switzerland
schwer	hard
schwimmen	swim (v)
segeln	sail (v)
sehen	see (v)
sehr schön	lovely
sehr	very
sein	be (v)
sein/e	his
Sekretär/in	secretary
selbe/r	same
selten	seldom
September	September
sich anmelden	register (v)
sich beeilen	hurry (v)
sich duschen	have a shower (v)
sich entschuldigen	apologise (v)
sich entspannen	relax (v)
sich setzen	take a seat (v)
sich sonnen	sunbathe (v)
sicher	safe/sure
Sicherheitsgurt	seat belt
sie (Mehrzahl)	they
Sie haben Glück	you are lucky
sie	she
Silvester	New Year's eve
sind	are
singen	sing (v)
sitzen	sit (v)
Sitzplatz	seat
Skifahren	ski (v)
so … wie	as … as
so bald wie möglich	asap = as soon as possible
so wie	like
Sohn	son
Sommer	summer
Sonne	sun
sonnig	sunny
Sonntag	Sunday
Soße	sauce
Spaß haben	have fun (v)

spät	late
später	later
Spaziergänge machen	go for walks (v)
Speisekarte	menu
speziell, besonders	special
Spiel	match
spielen	play (v)
Spieler/in	player
Sportler	sportsman
Sportlerin	sportswoman
Sportplatz	sports ground
sprechen	speak (v)
Stadion	stadium
Stadt	town/city
Stadtzentrum	city centre
stattfinden	take place (v)
Steckdose	socket
Stecker	plug
Stein	stone
Stellen Sie mich durch.	Put me through.
Stellen Sie sich vor.	Introduce yourself.
Stock/Stockwerke	floor
Stress	stress
Strich	dash
Stromversorger	electricity company
Student/in	student
Stuhl	chair
suchen	look for (v)
Supermarkt	supermarket
Suppe	soup
Tag	day
Tagesordnung	agenda
Tante	aunt
tanzen	dance (v)
Tasche	bag
Tasche	pocket
Tasse	cup
Taste (PC)	key
Techniker/in	technician
Tee	tea
telefonieren	phone (v)
Telefonnachricht	telephone message
Termin	appointment

teuer	expensive
Text	text
Theater	theatre
Tinte	ink
Tipp	tip
tippen	type (v)
Tisch	table
Toilette	toilet
Tomate	tomato
Torhüter	goalkeeper
tot	dead
treffen	meet (v)
trinken	drink (v)
Tschüss!	Cheerio!
tun	do (v)
Tür	door
Typ/Kollege	guy (slang)
typisch	typical
über/wegen	about
überprüfen	check (v)
übersetzen	translate (v)
Übersetzer/in	translator
überweisen	transfer (v)
Uhr	clock
Uhrzeit	time
um etwas bitten	ask for (something) (v)
Unabhängigkeit	independence
Universität	university
unser/e	our
Unterschrift	signature
unterstreichen	underline (v)
Unterstrich	underscore
Urlaub/Ferien	holiday
Vater	father
verbrauchen	use (v)
verdienen	earn (v)
vergessen	forget (v)
verheiratet	married
Verkauf	sale
verkaufen	sell (v)
Verkäufer	salesman
Verkäufer/in	shop assistant
Verkäuferin	saleswoman

Verkaufsabteilung	sales department
Verkaufsdirektor/in	sales director
verschieden	different
verstehen	understand (v)
versuchen	try (v)
Vetter/Kusine	cousin
Viele Grüße an ...	Give ... my love.
viele Leute	many people
Viertel	quarter
voll	full
von, aus	from
vor einer halben Stunde	half an hour ago
vor	before
vor	to
vorbei	past
vorbereiten	prepare (v)
vorgestern	the day before yesterday
Vorname	forename/first name
Vorspeise	starter
Vorwahl	dialling code
wählen	vote (v)
wählen (Telefon)	dial (v)
Wand	wall
Wann kann ich ihn erreichen?	When can I reach him?
war	was
waren	were
Warenhaus	department store
warm	warm
Warten Sie auf mich!	Wait for me!
warten	wait (v)
Was ist mit Musik?	What about music?
was	what
Wasser	water
Wasserfilter	water filter
Weg	way
Wein	wine
weiß	white
welche	which
Weltmeisterschaft	world cup
weniger	less
wenn möglich	if possible
wer	who
werden nicht	won't (will not)
wichtig	important
Wie bitte?	pardon?
Wie geht es Ihnen?	How are you?
Wie ist …?	What is … like?
Wie spät ist es?	What is the time?
wie	how
wiederholen	repeat
willkommen heißen	welcome (v)
Winter	winter
Wir freuen uns auf ihre Antwort.	We look forward to hearing from you.
Wir sehen uns.	See you.
wir	we
wirklich	really
wissen	know (v)
wo	where
Woche	week
Wochenende	weekend
Wohnung	flat
Wollen Sie warten?	Do you want to hold on?
Wurst	sausage
Zahl	figure
Zeit	time
Zeitung	newspaper
Zigarren	cigars
Zimmer	room (= hotel room)
zögern	hesitate (v)
zu Hause ankommen	get home (v)
zu Hause	at home
zu Tisch	at lunch
zu viele	too many
Zucker	sugar
zuhören	listen (v)
zum Beispiel	for example
zurück	back
zurückrufen	call back (v)
zuschauen	watch (v)
zweite/r	second

Selected Irregular Verbs

infinitive 1. Form	past tense 2. Form	past participle 3. Form	deutsche Bedeutung
let	let	let	(zu)lassen
lose	lost	lost	verlieren
be	was, were	been	sein
become	became	become	werden
begin	began	begun	beginnen
break	broke	broken	(zer)brechen
bring	brought	brought	(her)bringen
build	built	built	(er)bauen
buy	bought	bought	kaufen
catch	caught	caught	fangen
choose	chose	chosen	(aus)wählen
come	came	come	kommen
cost	cost	cost	kosten
cut	cut	cut	schneiden
deal	dealt	dealt	handeln
do	did	done	tun, machen
drink	drank	drunk	trinken
drive	drove	driven	fahren
eat	ate	eaten	essen
fall	fell	fallen	fallen
feel	felt	felt	(sich) fühlen
fight	fought	fought	kämpfen
find	found	found	finden
forget	forgot	forgotten	vergessen
get	got	got	bekommen
give	gave	given	geben
go	went	gone	gehen
grow	grew	grown	wachsen, ansteigen
hang	hung	hung	hängen
have	had	had	haben
hear	heard	heard	hören
hold	held	held	halten
keep	kept	kept	behalten
know	knew	known	wissen
lead	led	led	führen
leave	left	left	verlassen
lend	lent	lent	(ver)leihen

infinitive 1. Form	past tense 2. Form	past participle 3. Form	deutsche Bedeutung
make	made	made	machen, tun
mean	meant	meant	bedeuten
meet	met	met	treffen
pay	paid	paid	zahlen
put	put	put	setzen, stellen, legen
read	read	read	lesen
ride	rode	ridden	fahren, reiten
ring	rang	rung	anrufen, läuten
rise	rose	risen	(an)steigen
run	ran	run	laufen, betreiben
say	said	said	sagen
see	saw	seen	sehen
sell	sold	sold	verkaufen
send	sent	sent	schicken
show	showed	shown	zeigen
shut	shut	shut	schließen
sing	sang	sung	singen
sit	sat	sat	sitzen
sleep	slept	slept	schlafen
speak	spoke	spoken	sprechen
spend	spent	spent	verbringen, ausgeben
stand	stood	stood	stehen
steal	stole	stolen	stehlen
swim	swam	swum	schwimmen
take	took	taken	nehmen, dauern
teach	taught	taught	lehren
tell	told	told	erzählen
think	thought	thought	glauben, denken
throw	threw	thrown	werfen
understand	understood	understood	verstehen
wake	woke	woken	(er)wachen
wear	wore	worn	(Kleidung) tragen
win	won	won	gewinnen
write	wrote	written	schreiben